Engaging and Working with African American Fathers

Engaging and Working with African American Fathers: Strategies and Lessons Learned challenges traditional and historic practices and policies that have systematically excluded fathers and contributed to social and health disparities among this population.

With chapters written primarily by African American women – drawing on years of research, interviews, and practical experience with this demographic – each section explores current evidence on engagement approaches, descriptions of agencies/programs addressing specific issues fathers face, and case studies documenting typical clients and approaches to addressing their diverse needs. Offering an expansive overview of issues affecting African American fathers, the book explores important topics such as public, child and mental health, education, housing, and employment initiatives among others.

Engaging and Working with African American Fathers is a key resource for social work, public health, education students, researchers, practitioners, policymakers, and members of communities who are challenged by meeting the diverse needs of African American fathers.

Latrice S. Rollins is an Assistant Professor in the Department of Community Health and Preventive Medicine at Morehouse School of Medicine. She served as an enforcement/legal agent for the State of Georgia Department of Child Support Services for four years. Her specific focus on women in fatherhood and adding women's voices to the fatherhood field developed as a researcher and board member for the nonprofit organization Women in Fatherhood, Inc.

"Have we come to the conclusion that African American men are unwilling or unable to participate in the important work of child-rearing? Women certainly have a stake in the issue, and in *Engaging and Working with African American Fathers: Strategies and Lessons Learned* women take the lead to dispel this myth and clarify the social and policy reality of the vital work of engaging fathers. It is an essential contribution to fatherhood scholarship and analysis."

Jacquelyn Boggess, *Lecturer at University of Wisconsin School of Social Work and Executive Director at the Center for Family Policy & Practice*

"Rollins and her contributors have done a tremendous job in pulling together practices that will help to unify the current fragmented approaches to working with African American fathers. I would argue that this book must be regarded as a greatly important contribution to the fatherhood literature. It is invaluable for the manner in which authors combine the lessons learned on how to engage and work with both custodial and non-custodial fathers in the spheres of health, economics, and child development."

Obie Clayton, *Director of the Quality Enhancement Plan, ASA Edmond Ware Distinguished Professor in the Department of Sociology and Criminal Justice*

"This book is an impressive work by a team of extraordinary women! A must-read for fatherhood and family practitioners. The book illuminates the importance of understanding the challenges faced by African American fathers, yet, it also provides strategies for empowering them toward being the best fathers. This work is a genuine gift to the field of responsible fatherhood."

Jeffery Johnson, *President of the National Partnership for Community Leadership*

Engaging and Working with African American Fathers

Strategies and Lessons Learned

Edited by Latrice S. Rollins

Routledge
Taylor & Francis Group

NEW YORK AND LONDON

First published 2020
by Routledge
52 Vanderbilt Avenue, New York, NY 10017

and by Routledge
2 Park Square, Milton Park, Abingdon, Oxon, OX14 4RN

Routledge is an imprint of the Taylor & Francis Group, an informa business

© 2021 Taylor & Francis

Library of Congress Cataloging-in-Publication Data
Names: Rollins, Latrice S, editor.
Title: Engaging and working with African American fathers : strategies
and lessons / edited by Latrice S Rollins.
Description: 1 Edition. | New York City : Routledge Books, 2020. |
Includes bibliographical references and index.
Identifiers: LCCN 2020028940 (print) | LCCN 2020028941 (ebook) |
ISBN 9780367231200 (hardback) | ISBN 9780367231255 (paperback)
| ISBN 9780429278389 (ebook)
Subjects: LCSH: African American fathers.
Classification: LCC HQ756 .E535 2020 (print) | LCC HQ756 (ebook)
| DDC 306.874/208996073--dc23
LC record available at https://lccn.loc.gov/2020028940
LC ebook record available at https://lccn.loc.gov/2020028941

ISBN: 978-0-367-23120-0 (hbk)
ISBN: 978-0-367-23125-5 (pbk)
ISBN: 978-0-429-27838-9 (ebk)

Typeset in Bembo
by MPS Limited, Dehradun

Contents

Figures

Table

Foreword

In a post-civil rights, post-great recession, and currently, a depression-level economic status, crises abound. Within this backdrop, a deadly and unforgiving COVID-19 disease has penetrated and dominated the lives of people throughout the world community. Across America, however, a critical, timely, and ingenious conversation is occurring among thought leaders. Academicians; researchers; practitioners in geopolitical-economic domains, socio-religious, health, and social welfare systems professionals are re-examining the essence and necessity of fatherhood. Compelling messages from accomplished scholars, researchers, and practitioners are eloquently integrated into a carefully designed, well thought out framework, with commentary and critique about the necessity of healthy fatherhood. Numerous professionals across disciplines have written that fatherhood in America is at the crossroads, and this crisis has been lurking among families and communities for decades. The focus of this scholarly narrative judiciously addresses crises, challenges, and complexities. Collectively, these phenomena create the intersections that produce human and material systems that undergird the human condition. Still, roadmaps or blueprints with strategic plans and clearly defined actions are critical for the promulgation of better science and service about fatherhood. Individual, familial, organizational, and societal system levels are indispensable components needed for progress.

Engaging analytical discourse about fatherhood must begin with a review of and discussion about the family in the context of American history. Laws and policies that supported these practices over the centuries are well documented. Evidence about how indifference, harshness, and violence toward Black boys and men were allowed to exist for centuries needs to be confronted. Slavery, Redemption, Jim Crow, and the post-civil rights years have been unforgiving with longlasting burdens. Now, for starters, during the 21st century, a thorough and honest examination of brutalities against Black people must be discussed in the here and now before revisioning and reconstructing of the Black family can genuinely proceed.

Indeed, historical factors influenced the space, place, and status roles of marginalized, needful, and vulnerable families—and particularly Black boys and men. Black people, mostly men, transversed the Atlantic Ocean, forced—against their will, in chains, to satisfy the nation's labor workforce for the economic gain of White people and America. The production of rice, cotton, indigo, and other crops across the southern states helped to create enormous wealth for White slave owners. The economic stability of America is embedded in slavery and Jim Crow laws and practices. Similarly, Black women, although in smaller numbers, were also laborers who worked as hard and long in the fields as they did in the White masters' households. Recall that enslaved men and women were forcefully brought to America and sold as laborers. Their roles and responsibilities as heads of and creators and nurturers of families were never evident. Centuries later, once the slave trade began to diminish, the enslaved population increased because of rapes and breeding practices with enslaved Black women that were promulgated by White men. One component of these practices was to enlist Black men in the reproductive process, but without emotional attachments, caring, and long-term commitment to and respect for a family unit. Importantly, marriage between slaves was prohibited. However, enslaved men and women created secret rituals and ceremonies designed to demonstrate their commitment to and love for family structures. The significance of these relationships endured even when families had been torn apart and members were sold or traded. Secretly, some families were able to hold on to and nurture lasting relationships through underground communication systems developed by Black slaves.

The point here is that strong relationships and marriages were essential to Black people during the bitter and unforgiving centuries of slavery—the problematic years during Jim Crow, when lynching and other atrocities were common, continued for centuries. At one time in history, marriage rates were high, and relationships were sustained. During World War II, the marriage rates among Blacks were higher than those of their White counterparts. But things would change. Almost 80% of Blacks were married in 1950; in 1996, the rate was 34%. More recently, the marriage rate is estimated to about 26%. Of significance is the fact that 70% of Black children are being raised and nurtured in single parent, mostly father-absent homes. The custodial parent, usually the mother, is challenged and often overwhelmed by insufficient emotional and financial/material supports. Basic human needs, including adequate health care, housing, education, transportation, recreation, and safe environments are difficult to provide even with two parents in today's socioeconomic climates. Providing the necessities for a family can be insurmountable and sometimes impossible for a single parent. Fathers' absence matters! When will the nation seriously focus on the issues that are so well outlined in this critical work? *Turning the Corner on Father Absence in Black America*, as raised over two decades ago at the Morehouse Research Institute at Morehouse College, Atlanta, Georgia, could be a place to begin.

In this volume, stimulating, compelling paradigms for understanding the bases on which change can occur are presented by women who ingeniously connect historical struggles and recent issues to contemporary realities. They have identified ongoing concerns, made vital inquiry, and recommended actions based on best practices and culturally sensitive wisdom. Any review of significance and relevance about the Black experience in our nation must manifest thought leadership, knowledge and skills, courage, and tenacity. Black women have unstintingly guided the building and strengthening of families and communities. Black women have demonstrated a "being there" ethic and a commitment to their families, despite the backdrop of forced disconnection and separation. Fatherhood changes will require the relentless effort of Black women and men. Together, they must reinforce collective discipline. Over the centuries, women have responded to their individual and collective needs and the needs of men; most importantly, they nurtured and provided for the needs of children.

In keeping with the grand tradition of women's leadership and service, Latrice Rollins, PhD, presents this brilliant, valuable volume, *Engaging and Working with African American Fathers: Strategies and Lessons Learned*. She has added the voices of experts, women who have labored in the vineyard of fatherhood work for decades, to her voice—each one will provide leadership and expertise for each chapter. The science and scholarship that is evident in this distinguished work will influence theory and praxis for years to come.

References

Cruz, J. (2013). *Marriage: More than a century of change*. National Center for Family and Marriage Research: Bowling Green State University.

Franklin, R. (2007). *Crisis in the village. Restoring hope in African American communities*. Minneapolis: Fortress Press.

Gary, F.A., Yarandi, H., Hassan, M., Killion, C., Ncube, M., Still, C., & Hopps, J. (2019). A power conundrum: Black women and their sexual partners in the Midwest. *Issues in Mental Health Nursing*, 40(5), 431–436. doi:10.1080/01612840.2018.1547804.

Gilkes, C.T. (1998). Keeping faith with the people: Reflections on ethics, leadership and African American women's historical experience. In W.E. Flucker (Ed). *The stones that the builders rejected* (pp. 73–81). Harrisburg: Trinity Press International.

Hopps, J., Pinderhughes, E., & Shanker, R. (1995). *The power to care: Clinical practice effectiveness with overwhelmed clients*. New York: The Free Press.

Morehouse Research Institute (1998). *Turning the corner on father absence in Black America*. Atlanta: Morehouse College.

Acknowledgments

There are not enough words to express my gratitude to my sisters/ contributors and endorsers who helped to bring to fruition this overdue contribution to various disciplines. I appreciate these incredible authors for their support of my vision and willingness to share their practice wisdom and research findings. I am deeply grateful for Dr. June Gary Hopps' leadership, mentorship, and support. I thank my brothers who are leaders in the fatherhood field for embracing and advising me and endorsing this important work. I also acknowledge the fathers who shared their stories to serve as case studies for students and practitioners to learn how to better engage and work with them. Finally, I thank my father, Joseph Parnell, who inspires my fatherhood work; my mother, Germaine Harris, who encourages me to foster change; and my loving and supportive family, Shon, Sean, Seanna, and Solomon's Temple Christian Ministries.

Contributors

Tasha Alston, PhD, MSW, is an Assistant Professor at Western Carolina University in the College of Health and Human Services, Social Work Department in Cullowhee, NC, USA.

Tonya Boose, MPA, is the Director of the Veteran Program and Client Engagement Center of the Gateway Center in Atlanta, GA, USA.

Debra Beach Copeland, DNS, RN, CNE, is an Assistant Professor in Leadership & Advanced Nursing Practice, College of Nursing and Health Professions at The University of Southern Mississippi in Hattiesburg, MS, USA.

Ruby Norris Freeman, JD, is an attorney in Alexandria, LA, USA who has worked with the State of Louisiana and fatherhood programs and organizations.

Gina Green-Harris, MBA, is the Director of Milwaukee Outreach and Program Services in the Wisconsin Alzheimer's Institute at The University of Wisconsin School of Medicine and Public Health in Milwaukee, WI, USA.

June Gary Hopps, PhD, is the Thomas M. Parham Professor of Family and Children Studies at The University of Georgia School of Social Work in Athens, GA, USA.

Angelia O'Neal, MBA, is the CEO of M.E.N.S. Wear, Inc. in Atlanta, GA., USA.

Carmen Ray was a Parenting Facilitator with the Alma Center in Milwaukee, WI, USA.

Latrice Rollins, PhD, MSW, is an Assistant Professor at Morehouse School of Medicine in Department of Community Health & Preventive Medicine in Atlanta, GA, USA.

Petrice Sams-Abiodun, PhD, is the Vice President of External Services at Planned Parenthood Gulf Coast in New Orleans, LA, USA.

Diane Sears is an External Board Member at State Correctional Institute (SCI)-Phoenix Fathers and Children Together Initiative in Philadelphia, PA, USA.

Kisha Thomas, LPC, LPC, CPCS, ACS, EAS-C, is the Founder and Counselor at Max Empowerment, LLC in Atlanta, GA, USA.

1 Overview of Systemic Exclusion of African American Fathers and the Case for Engagement

Latrice Rollins

Introduction

The provision of social services to African American fathers has been an area of public interest and practice for decades (Mincy & Pouncy, 2002). This interest has developed in part because several studies have focused on the impact of fathers' active involvement in their children's lives. Father involvement and nurturance have been positively associated with children's intellectual development, social competence, internal locus of control, and ability to empathize and may protect children from the adverse effects of poverty, school problems, substance abuse, pregnancy, and crime (Huebner, Werner, Hartwig, White, & Shewa, 2008). The active involvement of fathers, particularly in the lives of African American children, has been an issue of public concern due to high disproportionate numbers of these children in foster care, living in poverty, and experiencing academic failure (Coakley, 2008; Sorenson & Zibman, 2001; Nord & West, 2001). Based on the father involvement literature, the effort to improve children's well-being has led to increased policies and programs focused on fathers. Specifically, due to high incarceration rates, high unemployment and jobless rates, low educational attainment, racism, and sexism, efforts to increase positive involvement of African American fathers requires special attention. In addition, a strengths-based perspective of African American fathers needs to be shared and embraced as African American fathers have been found to be more engaged in the lives of their children than any other group of men. African American fathers are diverse, and often their stories and images of their positive engagement and caregiving roles, despite the societal challenges, go unheard and unseen.

The majority of helping professionals are women, and there is some evidence that these professionals prevent African American fathers from receiving assistance and consequently serve as barriers to their involvement with their children (Coakley, 2008; Daniel & Taylor, 1999; Hamer & Marchioro, 2002; Huebner et al., 2008; O'Donnell, 1999). However, provision to this population by female practitioners will become more common. For example, 83% of licensed social workers are women and 70% of public health professionals are women (National Association of Social Workers, 2015; Association of Schools of Public

Health, 2006). In addition, African American women are more likely to be employed as officials and managers within helping professions. Despite the recent increase in numbers of female practitioners who provide services to men, the exclusion of African American fathers and the lack of knowledge about practice with this group have been identified as barriers to fathers' participation in services (Featherstone, 2001; Huebner et al., 2008; Sonenstein, Malm, & Billing, 2002). There is less empirical attention toward specific strategies female practitioners can employ to better engage this population. Many research studies suggest that more African American males should be hired as they share common backgrounds and experiences with these fathers (Anderson, Kohler, & Letiecq, 2002; Fletcher, Silberberg, & Baxter, 2001; Hopps, Pinderhughes, & Shankar, 1995; Jones, 2006). While this is needed, female service providers are the best available current options.

Numerous female practitioners have frequent contact with men as clients, and increased numbers of female practitioners have chosen to work with this population (Cree & Cavanagh, 1996; Pease, Camilleri, Pease, & Camilleri, 2001). The women that choose to work with African American fathers are unique as many social service agencies and professionals have excluded these fathers through various organizational policies and procedures and environments that center around motherhood (Rollins, 2010). While a number of studies, books, and reports exist on providing services to African American fathers, these studies fail to provide practice-based strategies that highlight predominantly female workforce creating successful helping alliances with this population. Therefore, the chapter authors are all women, predominately African American, who will share strategies that they employ to engage and work with African American fathers. The helping professions should be concerned with finding effective strategies to address the persistent needs of African American fathers and the professional development needs of emerging practitioners, particularly those who are women who will be working with these fathers. The professions' attention toward these issues will benefit students, practitioners, researchers, policy-makers, clients, and communities.

The Neglect of Scholarship on Practice with African American Fathers

The need for services for African American fathers should be a concern and priority for the helping professions given the research demonstrating their positive impact despite persistent social problems. African American fathers, particular those who are poor and unmarried, compose a group about whom students, practitioners, policymakers, or researchers are least aware (Gadsden, 2003). It is possible that a vicious cycle exists between education, practice, research, and policy in relation to effectively addressing the needs of African American fathers (Figure 1.1). There exists a cycle of exclusion that could be understood by systems theory, which assumes that these components, education, practice, research, and social

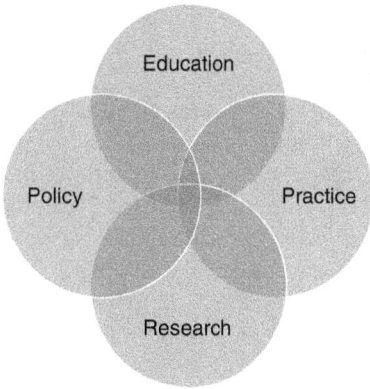

Figure 1.1 The Cycle of Exclusion of African American Fathers.

policy of our helping disciplines (i.e., public health, social work, medicine, education), compose a social system and are interrelated. Each component interacts with the other and change or (lack of change) in one component impacts the action (or lack of action) in the others. If a new social worker is not educated about the needs of African American fathers and how to address them, what would be his or her likelihood to engage these fathers in practice? If the social worker does not know how to engage African American fathers in practice, what would be the likelihood that he or she could conduct practice-based research with this population? If there are few to no practice-based research studies with African American fathers, what is the likelihood that proposed policies and programs will be reflective of the needs of this population and consequently their families? As systems theory assumes that one part of a system affects the whole, the exclusion of African American fathers in one component negatively impacts all—the lives of fathers, children, and families.

Education

Many staff lack the education and skills necessary to successfully connect fathers, especially African American fathers, to services (Huebner et al., 2008; O'Hagan, 1997; Sonenstein et al., 2002). However, there is a wealth of knowledge about African American fathers by African American scholars that can be used to educate students and current practitioners about practice with this population (Billingsley, 1992; Burgest, 1989; Freeman & Logan, 2004; Hopps & Pinderhughes, 1999; McAdoo, 2007; See, 2007). Researchers have also presented theories, programs, and practice guidelines that may be employed in order to ameliorate the practice with men (Allen & Gordon, 1990; Johnson, 2005) and specifically, the conditions of African American fathers (Behnke & Allen, 2007; Cochran, 1997; Davis, 1999; Dudley & Stone, 2001; Fagan & Hawkins, 2001; Mincy & Pouncy, 2002; Rasheed & Rasheed, 1999; Tuck, 1970). In the 1970s, African American social work scholars requested that the social work curriculum include more material on the Black community to respond to the changing societal conditions and knowledge base (Gary, 1973; Longres, 1973; Turner, 1973). However, this problem persists as the profession still fails to incorporate and further develop this material into social work education, practice, research, and policy.

Practice

Since few African American fathers have been involved in case assess-ments, case planning, or the receipt of services in child or public welfare systems, the opportunity to include them is missed in day-to-day practice (Coakley, 2008; Featherstone, 2001; O'Donnell, 1999; Rasheed & Stewart, 2007; Risley-Curtiss & Heffernan, 2003). The lack of basic demographic information or in-depth assessments with African American fathers in case records also reflects the failure to include them in the provision of services or refer them to programs (Huebner et al., 2008; O'Donnell, 1999; O'Hagan, 1997). To support African American fathers and families, the rhetoric of involving these fathers in health and human services must meet the realities of practice.

Research

Although there has been growth in the variety of services offered and in the diversity of individuals providing services to African American fathers, more research and evaluation of these programs are needed. The failure to evaluate and learn from practice with African American fathers not only risks the loss of scarce resources devoted to programs targeting this popu-lation, but the profession also neglects the opportunity to critically and effectively abolish the state of crisis some of these fathers and their families experience (Horn, 2003). The lack of research leads to the inability of policymakers to implement laws and policies that impact the circumstances surrounding these fathers. Ultimately, this perpetuates the cycle of exclusion, leading back to nonexistent or exclusive practices.

Policy

Historically, formal social service institutions have tended to systematically exclude African American families (Hopps & Lowe, 2008; Jewell, 1988; Roy, 2008). Since 1601, the *Elizabethan Poor Laws* set a precedent for government involvement in social service delivery. These laws mandated that communities assume responsibility for their poor and create institutions to care for the indigent (Jewell, 1988). African Americans have never been viewed as the deserving poor under these laws. All the major institutions of American society have failed to respond appropriately and effectively to the multiple needs and problems of African American men (Allen-Meares & Burman, 2003; Bronte-Tinkew, Bowie, & Moore, 2007; Gibbs, 1988; Sonenstein et al., 2002). Solomon (1988) suggests that public policy is the source of difficulties for African American males in social functioning. The role of the government has "historically stood as an obstacle to the freedom, independence, and opportunities available to African American families" (Billingsley, 1992, p. 76). Studies on responsible fatherhood programs present "compelling evidence that the nation's major social policies do not promote effective programming for young poor fathers" (Rasheed & Rasheed, 1999, p. 142). Regarding the lack of attention to the status of African American males, Allen-Meares and Burman (2003) stated "society's level of concern says much about us as a nation." Considerable apathy also exists about the plight of low-income African American men because of a belief system that purports that individuals who achieve great success do so because of their individual strengths such as motivation, dedication to the work ethic, and intelligence. Therefore, it is assumed that African American men do not deserve larger shares of the available services and resources (Solomon, 1988).

Throughout history, public policies have also been more supportive of motherhood than fatherhood, which has resulted in less access to services for fathers (Smith, 2004). Although sexism is usually not discussed in regard to African American fathers, it exists to prevent adequate service provision to them. Gendered obstacles are defined as "institutionally based racism and sexism that uniquely and profoundly impacts the availability of health and social services to African American men in America" (Rasheed & Stewart, 2007, p. 583). In 1952, Ralph Ellison addressed the psychological impact of racism on African American men when he wrote: "I am invisible, understand, simply because people refuse to see me." Chestang (1974) also stated "the reality of the black condition compels every black man to expend the majority of his energy in the struggle to survive. In every aspect of his life, the Black man wrestles daily with the choking tentacles of racism" (p. 395). Franklin and Boyd-Franklin (2000) presented a conceptual model to explain the impact of racism on African American men's behavior called the invisibility syndrome. The invisibility syndrome is defined as:

> The ongoing effort to manage racial slights, as well as the confusion and disillusionment induced by persistent acts of racism, [which] can undermine the resilience of some African Americans, leading to deterioration in their ability to cope, whether on a transient or a more enduring basis.
>
> (Franklin & Boyd-Franklin, 2000, p. 38)

Rasheed and Stewart (2007) also argued that the notion of negative invisibility, the process of the psychological and emotional experiences of African American males being rendered invisible, exists in the development and provision of social and mental health services. As a result, for decades, there were no "entirely federally funded or joint federal and state grant programs for low-income fathers" (Rasheed & Rasheed, 1999, p. 128).

Theoretical Perspectives

African American fathers are in many ways like all other American fathers but "because of history and contemporary social conditions, there are important differences" (Comer, 1989, p. 366). As all fathers may go to great lengths to fulfill their paternal roles, African American fathers are unique due to "the obstacles and weighty dilemmas of life for Black men [that] are produced and sustained primarily by the structure of American society itself" (Hamer, 2001, p. 2). Myrdal (1962) stated:

> [T]here is no single side of the Negro problem—whether it be the Negro's political status, the education he gets, his place in the labor market, his cultural and personality traits or anything else—which is not predominantly determined by its total American setting (p. lxxvii).

There is usually little regard for social context and sociocultural barriers that African American fathers face in performing their parental roles (Anderson & Letiecq, 2005). The forces of slavery, Jim Crow laws, and "new forms of inequities evolving within the context of an increasingly globalized economy and polity" (Booker, 2000, p. vii) must all be considered in a discussion of the needs of many African American fathers. African American scholars have developed multiple theoretical perspectives that could be used in the field to understand the issues that impact African American fatherhood (Billingsley, 1992; Chestang, 1976; Norton, 1978; Schiele, 1997). Although these theories seek to address the totality of the African American experience, they have yet to be fully integrated into education, practice, and research (Gilbert, Harvey, & Belgrave, 2009).

The ability to recognize the various influences and be flexible in practice is necessary in order for engagement with African American fathers to be successful. In this regard, Afrocentric, Black, dual, and holistic perspectives have been offered in the literature as guidance for practitioners to address the needs of this population, their families, and communities.

The Afrocentric Framework and Black Perspective

Afrocentric, Africentric, Afrocentricity, and African-centered perspective are interchangeable terms used to describe a framework that puts African American lives, values, culture, and history at the center of analysis

(Graham, 1999). This perspective was offered as an alternative to Eurocentric theories or worldviews that emphasize "linear, individualistic, materialistic, rationalistic understanding of human beings and reality in general" (Schiele, 1997, p. 802). Also, it was stated that the European perspective results in creating false dichotomies that might not be applicable to the African American experience (Jackson, 1976). As there are many names for the perspective, there are also several different definitions and assumptions depending on the author. The central assumption of the Afrocentric perspective is that human and societal problems in the United States originate from "oppression and spiritual alienation" (Schiele, 1997). Another assumption is that the "philosophical integrity of traditional Africa has survived among continental Africans and slavery and the denial of African culture did not destroy all of the cultural vestiges of Africa in African Americans" (Schiele, 1997, p. 284). Therefore, this worldview emphasizes that African principles or values should be used to understand African American behavior. The four themes of the Afrocentric perspective are interdependency, collectivity, spirituality, and affect (Schiele, 2000b). The Black perspective is a similar philosophical stance that, in addition to those themes listed above, also promotes family, self-determination, life, dignity, brotherhood, self-sufficiency, and Black identity (Chunn, 1974, p. 18).

The majority of studies that have examined the Afrocentric perspective as a framework for programs involve African American youth and reported positive outcomes in social skill development and anger management (Banks, Hogue, Timberlake & Liddle, 1996; Moore, Madison-Colmore, & Moore, 2003). There are also a few studies on practice with African American fathers that recommend the use of Afrocentric values, particularly the emphasis on family and community responsibilities (Levine & Pitt, 1995; Rasheed & Johnson, 1995).

However, there are more conceptual publications than empirical on the use of this perspective and no empirical support exists to identify observed Afrocentric values (Bush, 1999; Mazama, 2001). It is difficult to assess the difference between Afrocentric values and ethical responsibilities of practice, such as self-determination and the importance of human relationships, or the difference between Afrocentric interventions and those that are called "culturally appropriate" or "culturally sensitive." This is especially difficult when some scholars state that Afrocentric practice can be applied to practice with other racial/ethnic populations (Karenga, 1993; Kershaw, 1992; Schiele, 1997). This has complicated empirical testing of the assumptions of the Afrocentric perspective and replication of studies utilizing the Afrocentric perspective as a framework.

The assumption that a core Afrocentric value system exists among Africans and African Americans is often criticized for asserting the superiority of the African race and at the same time minimizing the agency of African Americans (Cobb, 1997). The existence of "idealized" Afrocentric values has also been criticized in light of the atrocities committed by Africans against other Africans, including those who participated in the kidnapping and selling of Africans into the Atlantic slave trade. However, Nobles and Goddard (1993) counter this critique by stating that culture and behavior are separate. Therefore, while problem behaviors exist among Africans and African Americans, these authors state that destructive behavior is not an expression of the values of the culture:

> It is important to remember that current behavior results from the interaction of the culture and the material condition of a people and that both, culture and condition, must be understood and manipulated if interventions and change is to be achieved. (p. 117)

The rationale for the development of an Afrocentric perspective is understood. Many Eurocentric theories have been used in various disciplines that emphasized the genetic inferiority of African Americans and blamed the issues that African Americans faced on individual deficits. Therefore, African American scholars recognized the need to emphasize the strengths of African Americans and address the oppression that the population faces. There is certainly a need to understand African American fathers outside of a Western, traditional, or mainstream paradigm. Studies have found that due to the fact that most African American mothers and fathers share family responsibilities in providing and caring for children, research and interventions should not be based on the same theories used for traditional nuclear families (Burlew, Banks, McAdoo, & Azibo, 1992; See, 2007).

Dual Perspective

In practice, the dual perspective could be used to understand the experiences of African American fathers. The dual perspective originated with DuBois' concept of "double consciousness." DuBois (1903) stated "one ever feels his twoness, an American, a Negro; two souls, two thoughts, two unreconciled strivings; two warring ideals in one dark body, whose dogged strength alone keeps it from being torn asunder." Chestang (1976) further developed the notion of twoness that African Americans experience in relation to their environment. While individuals are all a part of two systems, one which is the larger society and the other the "immediate physical and social environment" (Norton, 1978, p. 3), there is a difference in the way that these environments are experienced by African Americans. The two environments are called the sustaining and nurturing environments. Chestang (1974) stated:

> The sustaining environment consists of the survival needs of man—goods and services, political power, economic resources; larger society makes an instrumental adaptation to it, hostility in the

sustaining environment; the nurturing environment, the black community–individual emotional support, cultural values, family relationships and supportive institutions, relationship to this world is expressive (sense of wholeness and identification). (p. 70)

Thus, Norton (1978) defined the dual perspective as:

The conscious and systematic process of perceiving, understanding, and comparing simultaneously the values, attitudes, and behavior of the larger societal system with those of the client's immediate family and community system. (p. 3)

The dual perspective is not only useful in understanding systems and the impact on African Americans but individuals of various ethnic/racial backgrounds (Brown, 1978; Murase, 1978; Valle, 1978). Therefore, the dual perspective is used to assess issues presented by the client specifically by analyzing the incongruency that individuals may experience as they try to maneuver their existence through these two systems (Norton, 1978). Practitioners should understand that the double consciousness is expressed as a tool of survival because it may seem that African Americans only have two choices: "succumb to the erosive denials of his humanity or perform adaptive maneuvers to preserve his integrity" (Chestang, 1974, p. 70). By also challenging staff to become aware of their own value systems, the dual perspective is a means for practitioners to provide services free of the "stereotyping, misinterpretations, incorrect expectations, and inappropriate interventions" (Norton, 1978, p. 3) that African American fathers might typically encounter when seeking services. Norton (1978) refers to this ability as having a reversible mind, having the ability and "conscious motivation" to examine the relationship between larger society and immediate environment, their own values, and the knowledge to guide interventions and actions (p. 12).

Holistic Perspective

A holistic understanding of the difficulties contemporary African American fathers face requires attention to culture, history, and contemporary society (Billingsley, 1992; Hamer & Marchioro, 2002; Roberts, 1998). Figure 1.2 is an adoption of Billingsley's (1992) holistic model for African American families. In addition to history and various social relationships, this figure demonstrates that African American fathers specifically have to be understood through their interactions within communities and society. The community consists of churches, schools, business enterprises, and voluntary organizations. Society includes a number of systems but has been categorized as government, private business, voluntary, nonsectarian, and religious sectors (Billingsley, 1992). Boyd-Franklin (2003) adds that while

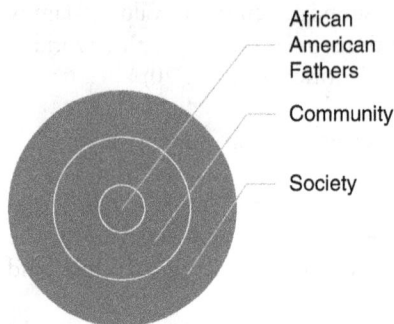

Figure 1.2 The Holistic Perspective. Adopted from Billingsley (1992).

there are multiple issues, the various systems involved must be a part of the solution. This understanding, if grasped by practitioners, educators, researchers, and policymakers, would alter current ineffective approaches to the problems (Franklin, 1997; Hamer & Marchioro, 2002).

In summary, each of these perspectives has been offered by African American scholars as a way to understand and guide practice with African Americans. The dual and holistic perspectives are more grounded in systems theory and offer ways to examine the African American fathers' total experience in community and society. Despite its critics, scholars who support the Afrocentric perspective state that research and practice with African American fathers should not be guided by Western, Eurocentric theories that have been known to perpetuate negative images and stereotypes of nontraditional family forms.

While the focus of the research on African American men in the 1990s was on problems, the millennium must bring solutions to address the needs of this population. There may be hope in store as there continues to be an increase in knowledge about the experiences of men as demonstrated by the rise in men's studies (Gordon, 2004). The historical difficulties this population has faced must be understood by practitioners seeking to engage this population. In addition, the joining of skill and cultural competence will advance practice with African American fathers.

As evidenced by the literature reviewed in this chapter, our society has created and reinforced several barriers that effectively reduce fathers' involvement with their children and families (Parke & Brott, 1999). A multidimensional understanding of these fathers is essential to advancing practice, education, and research. Although we are behind in developing empirically based strategies to engage African American fathers, the literature reveals many areas that have been explored that offer opportunities for the profession to begin engaging with this population (Dudley & Stone, 2001; Hopps et al. 1995; Rasheed & Rasheed, 1999; See, 2007). Clark and Hopkins (1969) stated:

[S]ocial agencies must have courage to reexamine ruthlessly their present assumptions, methods, and programs and prune those postures and pretenses which reflect only traditional and bureaucratic lags or fundraising gimmicks. Must dare to run the risks of being part of a real and comprehensive program of social action and social change. (p. 50)

Now is the opportunity to lead the discourse on the complexities of practice with African American fathers while social and political attention is focused on the systemic inequities this population faces. The combination of over three decades of scholarly dialogue on father involvement and the recent opportunities presented by federal initiatives make it possible for staff and students to develop the skills and resources and move toward father-inclusive services (Featherstone, 2001; Kruk, 1994).

It is hoped that the experiences of the chapter authors, women who are engaging and working with African American fathers, will add to minimal existing knowledge about engaging and working with fathers and the lessons learned. Each chapter contains a case that describes an African American father, his reason for receiving services, and the strategies implemented with the client. Cases were not meant to be generalizable as African American fathers are diverse and not limited to one situation or "snapshot." All client/participant names and some organization names have been changed or not provided for confidentiality purposes. Overall, the cases reflect the broad scope of services needed and received by African American fathers.

Reflection on cases allows staff and students to learn how to handle similar cases more effectively (Flyvbjerg, 2011; McCoyd & Kerson, 2016). Research with helping professionals indicates that building professional confidence takes time, primarily time for reflecting on cases (Bischoff & Barton, 2002). This type of reflection is critical to deep learning and professional development (Epstein, Siegel, & Silberman, 2008; McCoyd & Kerson, 2016). Reflection and discussion of the cases will help staff and students enhance their expertise and increase their awareness of ways that they may have addressed the cases in their context. The use of cases allows context-rich knowledge to be shared with students and staff while challenging those seasoned in the field to think more deeply about how practice may have been improved (McCoyd & Kerson, 2016).

References

Allen, J., & Gordon, S. (1990). Creating a framework for change. In R.L. Meth & R.S Pasick (Eds.), *Men in therapy: The challenge of change* (pp. 131–151). New York: The Guilford Press.

Allen-Meares, P., & Burman, S. (2003). The endangerment of African American men: An appeal for social work action. In O. Harris & R. Miller (Eds.), *Impacts of incarceration on the African American family* (pp. 187–198). New Brunswick, NJ: Transaction Publishers.

Anderson, E.A., Kohler, J.K., & Letiecq, B.L. (2002). Low-income fathers and "responsible fatherhood programs": A qualitative investigation of participants' experiences. *Family Relations*, 51(2), 148–155.

Anderson, E.A., & Letiecq, B.L. (2005). Situating fathers in responsible fatherhoodprograms: A place to explore father identity. In Marsiglio W., Roy K., & Fox G.L. (Eds.), *Situated fathering: A focus on physical and social spaces* (pp. 187–208). Lanham, MD: Rowman & Littlefield Publishers, Inc.

Association of Schools of Public Health. (2006). Retrieved from https://www.aspph.org/.

Banks, R., Hogue, A., Timberlake, T., & Liddle, H. (1996). An Afrocentric approach to group social skills training with inner-city African-American adolescents. *Journal of Negro Education*, 65, 414–423.

Behnke, A.O., & Allen, W.D. (2007). Effectively serving low-income fathers of color. *Marriage & Family Review*, 42(2), 29–50.

Billingsley, A. (1992). *Climbing Jacob's ladder: The enduring legacy of African American families*. New York: Simon & Schuster.

Bischoff, R.J., & Barton, M. (2002). The pathway toward clinical self-confidence. *The American Journal of Family Therapy*, 30, 231–242.

Booker, C.B. (2000). *'I will wear no chain!': A social history of African American males*. Santa Barbara, CA: Greenwood Publishing Group.

Bronte-Tinkew, J., Bowie, L., & Moore, K. (2007). Fathers and public policy. *Applied Development Science*, 11(4), 254–259.

Boyd-Franklin, N. (2003). *Black families in therapy: Understanding the African American experience*. New York.

Brown, E.F. (1978). American Indians in modern society: Implications for social policy and services. In D.G. Norton (Ed.), *Inclusion of ethnic minority content in the social work curriculum* (pp. 68–80). New York: Council on Social Work Education.

Burgest, D.R. (1989). *Social work practice with minorities*. Metuchen, N.J.: The Scarecrow Press.

Burlew, A.K.H., Banks, W.C, McAdoo, H.P., & Azibo, D.A. (1992). *African American psychology: Theory, research, and practice*. Newbury Park, CA: Sage Publications, Inc.

Bush, L.V. (1999). Am I a man?: A literature review engaging sociohistorical dynamics of Black manhood in the United States. *The Western Journal of Black Studies*, 23(1), 49–57.

Chestang, L.W. (1974). The issue of race in social work practice. In P.E. Weinberger (Ed.), *Perspectives on social welfare: An introductory anthology* (2nd ed., pp. 393–402). New York: Macmillan Publishing Co., Inc.

Chestang, L. (1976). Environmental influences on social functioning: The Black experience. In Cafferty P. S. J., & Chestang L., (Eds.), *The diverse society: Implications for social policy* (pp. 59–74). Washington, DC: National Association of Social Workers.

Chunn, J. (1974). Integrating minority content into the social work curriculum: A model based on Black perspective and principles. In Council of Social Work Education (Ed.), *Black perspectives on social work education: Issues related to curriculum, faculty, and students* (pp. 13–25). New York: Council on Social Work Education.

Clark, K.B, & Hopkins, J. (1969). *A relevant war against poverty: A study of community action programs and observable social change*. New York: Harper & Row Publishers.

Coakley, T.M. (2008). Examining African American fathers' involvement in permanency planning: An effort to reduce racial disproportionality in the child welfare system. *Child and Youth Services Review*, 30, 407–417.

Cobb, W. (1997). Out of Africa: The dilemmas of Afrocentricity. *The Journal of Negro History*, 82(1), 122–132.

Cochran, D.L. (1997). African American fathers: A decade review of the literature. *Families in Society*, 78(4), 340–350.

Comer, J.P. (1989). Black fathers. In S.H. Cath, A. Gurwitt & L. Gunsberg Eds., *Fathers and families* (pp. 365–383). Hillsdale, NJ: The Analytic Press.

Cree, V.E., & Cavanagh, K. (1996). Men, masculinism and social work. In K. Cavanaugh & V.E Cree (Eds.), *Working with men: Feminism and social work* (pp. 1–8). New York: Routledge.

Daniel, B., & Taylor, J. (1999). The rhetoric versus the reality: A critical perspective on practice with fathers in child care and protection work. *Child & Family Social Work*, 4(3), 209–220.

Davis, L. (1999). *Working with African American males*. Thousand Oaks, CA: Sage Publications.

DuBois, W.E.B. (1903). *The souls of black folk*. New York: Oxford University Press.

Dudley, J.R, & Stone, G. (2001). *Fathering at risk: Helping nonresidential fathers*. New York: Springer Publishing Company, Inc.

Epstein, R.M., Siegel, D.J., & Silberman, J. (2008). Self-monitoring in clinical practice: A challenge for medical educators. *Journal of Continuing Education in the Health Professions*, 28, 5–13.

Fagan, J., & Hawkins, A.J. (2001). *Clinical and educational interventions with fathers*. New York: The Haworth Clinical Press.

Featherstone, B. (2001). Putting fathers on the child welfare agenda. *Child and Family Social Work*, 6, 179–186.

Fletcher, R., Silberberg, S., & Baxter, R. (2001). *Father's access to family-related services*. New South Wales, Australia: Family Action Centre.

Flyvbjerg, B. (2011). Case study. In N.K. Denzin & Y.S. Lincoln (Eds.), *The sage handbook of qualitative research* (4th Ed., pp. 301–316). Thousand Oaks, CA: Sage.

Franklin, A.J., & Boyd-Franklin, N. (2000). Invisibility syndrome: A clinical model of the effects of racism on African American males. *American Journal of Orthopsychiatry*, 70(1), 33–41.

Franklin, D.L. (1997). *Ensuring inequality: The structural transformation of the African American family*. New York: Oxford University Press.

Freeman, E.M., & Logan, S.L. (2004). Common heritage and diversity among Black families and communities: An Africentric research paradigm. In E.M. Freeman & S. L. Logan (Eds.), *Reconceptualizing the strengths and common heritage of Black families: Practice, research, and policy issues* (pp. 5–24). Springfield, IL: Charles C. Thomas.

Gadsden, V.L. (2003). Expanding the concept of "family" in family literacy: Integrating a focus on fathers. In A. Debruin-Parecki & B. Kroll-Sinclair (Eds.), *Family literacy: From theory to practice* (pp. 86–125). Newark, DE: International Reading Association.

Gary, L.E. (1973). Social work education and the Black community: A proposal for curriculum revisions. In J.A Goodman (Ed.), *Dynamics of racism in social work practice* (pp. 316–329). Washington, D.C: National Association of Social Workers, Inc.

Gibbs, J.T (1988). Young Black males in America: Endangered, embittered, and embattled. In J. Gibbs (Ed.), *Young, Black, and male in America: An endangered species* (pp. 1–36). Dover, MA: Auburn House Publishing Company.

Gilbert, D.J, Harvey, A.R., & Belgrave, F.Z. (2009). Advancing the Africentric paradigm shift discourse: Building toward evidence-based Africentric interventions in social work practice with African Americans. *Social Work*, 54(3), 243–253.

Gordon, J. (2004). *The Black male in White America*. New York: Nova Science Publishers.

Graham, M.J. (1999). The African-centered worldview: Toward a paradigm for social work. *Journal of Black Studies*, 30(1), 103–122.

Hamer, J. (2001). *What it means to be daddy: Fatherhood for Black men living away from their children*. New York: Columbia University Press.

Hamer, J., & Marchioro, K. (2002). Becoming custodial dads: Exploring parenting among low-income and working class African American fathers. *Journal of Marriage and the Family*, 64(1), 116–129.

Hopps, J.G., & Lowe, T.B. (2008). The scope of social work practice. In K.M. Sowers, C.N. Dulmus (Vol Eds.) & B. White (Section Ed.), *Comprehensive handbook of social work and social welfare, Vol. 1: The profession of social work* (pp. 37–64). New York: John Wiley & Son, Inc.

Hopps, J.G., & Pinderhughes, E. (1999). *Group work with overwhelmed clients: How the power of groups can help people transform their lives*. New York: The Free Press.

Hopps, J.G, Pinderhughes, E., & Shankar, R. (1995). *The power to care: Clinical practice effectiveness with overwhelmed clients*. New York: The Free Press.

Horn, W.F. (2003). Is it working? Early evaluations of fatherhood-renewal programs. In O. Clayton, R.B. Mincy & D. Blankenhorn (Eds.), *Black fathers in contemporary American society: Strengths, weaknesses, and strategies for change* (pp. 138–152). New York: Russell Sage Foundation.

Huebner, R.A, Werner, M., Hartwig, S., White, S., & Shewa, D. (2008). Engaging fathers: Needs and satisfaction in child protective services. *Administration in Social Work*, 32(2), 87–103.

Jackson, G.G. (1976). The African genesis of the Black perspective in helping. *Professional Psychology*, 7(3), 292–308. Retrieved from https://doi.org/10.1037/0735-7028.7.3.292.

Jewell, K.S. (1988). *Survival of the Black family: The institutional impact of U.S. social policy*. New York: Praeger Publishers.

Johnson, N.G. (2005). Women helping men: Strengths and barriers to women therapists working with men clients. In G.E. Good & G.R Brooks (Eds.), *The new handbook of psychotherapy and counseling with men: A comprehensive guide to settings, problems, and treatment approaches* (pp. 291–307). San Francisco, CA: Jossey-Bass.

Jones, C. (2006). Fatherhood training: The Concordia project. In M.E Connor & J.L. White (Eds.), *Black fathers: An invisible presence in America* (pp. 243–255). Mahwah, NJ: Lawrence Erlbaum Associates, Inc.

Karenga, M. (1993). *Introduction to black studies* (2nd ed.). Los Angeles: University of Sankore Press.

Kershaw, T. (1992). Afrocentrism and the Afrocentric method. *The Western Journal of Black Studies*, 16(3), 160–168.

Kruk, E. (1994). The disengaged noncustodial father: Implications for social work practice with the divorced family. *Social Work*, 39(1), 15–25.

Levine, J.A., & Pitt, E.W. (1995). *New expectations: Community strategies for responsible fatherhood*. New York: Families and Work Institute.

Longres, J. (1973). The impact of racism on social work education. *Journal of Education for Social Work*, 8(1), 31–41.

Mazama, A. (2001). The Afrocentric paradigm: Contours and definitions. *Journal of Black Studies*, 31(4), 387–405.

McAdoo, H.P. (2007). *Black families*. Thousand Oaks, CA: Sage Publications, Inc.

McCoyd, J.L., & Kerson, T.S. (2016). *Social work in health settings: Practice in context.* Routledge.

Mincy, R.B., & Pouncy, H.W. (2002). The responsible fatherhood field: Evolution and goals. In C.S. Tamis-LeMonda & N. Cabrera (Eds.), *Handbook of father involvement: Multidisciplinary perspectives* (pp. 555–597). Mahwah, NJ: Lawrence Erlbaum Associates.

Moore, S.E., Madison-Colmore, O., & Moore, J.L. (2003). An Afrocentric approach to substance abuse treatment with adolescent African American males: Two case examples. *The Western Journal of Black Studies, 27,* 219–230.

Murase, K. (1978). Social welfare policy and services: Asian Americans. In D.G. Norton (Ed.), *Inclusion of ethnic minority content in the social work curriculum* (pp. 34–47). New York: Council on Social Work Education.

Myrdal, G. (1962). *An American dilemma: The Negro problem and modern democracy.* New York: Harper & Row Publishers, Inc.

National Association of Social Workers (2015). *Assuring the sufficiency of a frontline workforce: A national study of licensed social workers.* Retrieved from http://www.socialworkers.org.

Nobles, W.W., & Goddard, L.L. (1993). An African-centered model of prevention for African-American youth at high risk. In L.L. Goddard (Ed.), *An African-Centered model of prevention for African-American youth at high risk* (pp. 114–128). Rockville, MD: Center for Substance Abuse Prevention.

Nord, C.W., & West, J. (2001). *Fathers' and mothers' involvement in their children's schools by family type and resident status.* Washington, D.C.: United States Department of Education, National Center for Education Statistics.

Norton, D. (1978). *The dual perspective: Inclusion of ethnic minority content in the social work curriculum.* New York: Council on Social Work Education.

O'Donnell, J.M. (1999). Involvement of African American fathers in kinship foster care services. *Social Work, 44,* 428–441.

O'Hagan, K. (1997). The problem of engaging men in child protection work. *The British Journal of Social Work, 27*(1), 25–42.

Parke, R.D., & Brott, A.A. (1999). *Throwaway dads: The myths and barriers that keep men from being the fathers they want to be.* Boston: Houghton Mifflin Company.

Pease, B., & Camilleri, P. (Eds.). (2001). Feminism, masculinity politics and the human services. In *Working with men in the human services* (pp. 1–11). Crow's Nest, Australia: Allen & Unwin.

Rasheed, J.M., & Johnson, W.E. (1995). Non-custodial African American fatherhood: A case study research approach. *Journal of Community Practice, 2*(2), 99–116.

Rasheed, J.M., & Rasheed, M.N. (1999). *Social work practice with African American men: The invisible presence.* Thousand Oaks, CA: Sage Publications.

Rasheed, J.M., & Stewart, R. (2007). The impact of racism, poverty, educational attainment, and masculine identity on the efficacy of African American fatherhood. In L. See (Ed.), *Human behavior in the social environment from an African American perspective* (pp. 565–587). New York: Haworth Press.

Risley-Curtiss, C., & Heffernan, K. (2003). Gender biases in child welfare. *Affilia, 18*(10), 1–15.

Rollins, L.S. (2010). *An exploration of the experiences of African American women who provide direct services to African American nonresidential fathers* (Doctoral dissertation, uga). Retrieved from https://getd.libs.uga.edu/pdfs/rollins.

Roberts, D. (1998). The absent Black father. In C.R. Daniels (Ed.), *Lost fathers: The politics of fatherlessness in America* (pp. 145–161). New York: St. Martin's Press.

Roy, K. (2008). A life course perspective on fatherhood and family policies in the United States and South Africa. *Fathering: A journal of theory research & practice about men as fathers*, 6(2), 92–112.

See, L.A. (2007). *Human behavior in the social environment from an African-American perspective* (2nd ed.). Binghamton, NY: The Haworth Press, Inc.

Schiele, J.H. (1997). The contour and meaning of Afrocentric social work. *Journal of Black Studies*, 27(6), 800–819.

Schiele, J.H. (2000a). Challenges and opportunities of the Personal Responsibility Act for African American families and communities. In L.G. Nackerud & M. Robinson (Eds.), *Early implications of welfare reform in the southeast* (pp. 137–150). Huntington, NY: Nova Science Publishers, Inc.

Schiele, J.H. (2000b). *Human services and the Afrocentric paradigm*. Binghamton, NY: Haworth Press.

Smith, J.M. (2004). The demography of African American families and children at the end of the 20th century. In J.E. Everett, S.P. Chipungu, & B.R. Leashore (Eds.), *Child welfare revisited: An Africentric perspective* (pp. 15–56). New Brunswick, NJ: Rutgers University Press.

Solomon, B. (1988). The impact of public policy on the status of young Black males. In J. Gibbs (Ed.), *Young, Black, and male in America: An endangered species* (pp. 294–316). Dover, MA: Auburn House Publishing Company.

Sonenstein, R., Malm, K., & Billing, A. (2002). *Study of fathers' involvement in permanency planning and child welfare casework*. Washington, D. C.: United States Department of Health and Human Services.

Sorenson, E., & Zibman, C. (2001). Poor dads who don't pay child support: Deadbeats or disadvantaged? *Social Service Review*, 75, 420–434.

Tuck, S. (1970). A model for working with Black fathers. *Research Report*, 6(11), 1–13.

Turner, J.B. (1973). Education for practice with minorities. In J.A. Goodman (Ed.), *Dynamics of racism in social work practice* (pp. 306–316). Washington, D.C: National Association of Social Workers, Inc.

Valle, R. (1978). The development of a polycultural social policy curriculum from the Latino perspective. In Norton D.G., (Ed.), *Inclusion of ethnic minority content in the social work curriculum* (pp. 64–74). New York: Council on Social Work Education.

2 Engaging and Working with African American Fathers in Maternal and Child Health

This study was funded by the W. K. Kellogg Foundation

Debra Beach Copeland and Petrice Sams-Abiodun

Introduction

Becoming a father can be a stressful, transitional event in the lives of new fathers (Asenhed, Kilstam, Alehagen, & Baggens, 2013; Giallo et al., 2015), who are often not prepared to assume the father role (Dayton et al., 2016). But unlike mothers, fathers' needs are rarely addressed in maternal and child health (MCH) systems or health care environments, which leads to fathers, especially low-income fathers, facing many challenges in accessing services to meet their needs in their new father role (Gadsden, Ford, & Breiner, 2016; Lu et al., 2010). Due to racial discrimination in US systems, for example, in housing, health care, and criminal justice, fathers in African American families may have more difficulty accessing resources to help them transition and develop their father role (Lu et al., 2010). Studies show that fathers want to be productive and nurturing in the father role, and early parenting periods are ideal times when practitioners can help fathers develop positive parenting behaviors that support their infants' development (Dayton et al., 2016; Giallo et al., 2015; Smith, Tandon, Blair-Merritt, & Hanson, 2015). Moreover, father involvement in families is very important to the general health and well-being of mothers and children (Davis, Vyankandondera, Luchters, Simon, & Holmes, 2016; Tokki et al., 2018).

Since fathers have little formal preparation for becoming a father, they may need more social support resources to facilitate their adaptations to the father role (Giallo et al., 2015; Henshaw et al., 2018; Murphy, Gordon, Sherrod, Dancy, & Kershaw, 2012; Seymour, Dunning, Cooklin, & Giallo, 2014). It is important to support fathers, whether they are new or experienced fathers. Social networks are very important in supporting fathers in their new father role (Murphy et al., 2012). However, many health care professionals and community organizations may not implement father-friendly practices or address fathers' infant caretaking concerns in well-baby visits or office meetings (Carlson, Edleson, & Kimball, 2014). Therefore, the purpose of this descriptive, qualitative study is to describe how social networks, health care professionals, and community organizations provide social support to new and experienced urban fathers during the first year of birth of their infants.

MCH and Fathers

The mission of MCH programs is to improve the health of mothers, infants and children (Healthy People, 2020). However, many federal agencies and national organizations stress the importance of involving fathers in maternal and child care (Association of Maternal & Child Health Programs [AMCHP], 2009; Maternal and Child Health Bureau [MCHB] of the Health Resources & Services Administration [HRSA], 2020; National Healthy Start Association, 2015). In a recent systematic review of father involvement on maternal and newborn health, researchers found that fathers significantly impacted the health of mothers and infants by providing financial and emotional support and helping mothers and infants access health care services. In addition, fathers' involvement in maternal and newborn health improves couple relationships, too (Tokki et al., 2018). Further, father involvement has been associated with influencing the infant's cognitive, socio-emotional, physical, and developmental outcomes (Bronte-Tinkew, Carrano, Horowitz, & Kinkawa, 2008; Lamb, 2010) and facilitating neurodevelopment in early infancy (Kim, Kang, Yee, Shim, & Chung, 2016). Moreover, researchers have found that father's parenting skills sensitive to the child's emotional and developmental needs influence the child's executive functioning and the ability to solve problems at three years of age (Towe-Goodman et al., 2014).

Traditionally, fathers have not been included in MCH, and service providers have not focused on the father's needs during prenatal, post-partum, and well-child check-ups (Commission on Paternal Involvement in Pregnancy Outcomes [CPIPO], 2009; Garfield & Isacco, 2006). Are fathers' roles in the 21st century essential or accessory? This was the topic of an editorial in which Martin and Redshaw (2010) explored the positive impact of fathers on families and the development of healthy infants and children. It is important to focus on families as a whole and to promote and expect father involvement in the care of their children, starting in pregnancy, childbirth, and early infancy (Alio, Lewis, Scarborough, Harries, & Fiscella, 2013; Bond, 2010; CPIPO, 2009; Yogman & Garfield, 2016).

Social Support Needs of African American Fathers

The conceptual framework for the study is based on House's (1981) Social Support Theory. Social support is defined as the perception that one is cared for, receives assistance from other people, and has linkages to other social networks who may or may not provide social support or serve another function other than social support. Four types of social support are identified in this theory: (1) emotional support (expressions of empathy, love, trust, and caring), (2) instrumental support (tangible aid and services), (3) informational support (advice, suggestions, and information), and (4) appraisal support (information that is useful for self-evaluation). Two types of informal social networks include informal networks (for example, family and friends) and formal networks (for example, professionals like doctors, nurses, and social workers), and formalized groups or organizations that provide services (for example, clinics, nonprofits, and churches).

Fathers receive social support when they receive assistance from others through social relationships, such as receiving aid from grandparents or neighbors, or through interpersonal transactions, such as taking their infant to the pediatrician's office for well-child visits (Murphy et al., 2012). The father-infant relationship is very important to supporting positive infant outcomes. As fathers become more engaged with their infants, they turn to family members and friend networks for assistance in helping them take care of them (Lamb, 2010). Smaller networks provide better support for fathers, especially for helping fathers deal with unhelpful behaviors and peer pressure (Murphy et al., 2012). In fact, fathers usually ask a small group of family and friends for parenting information and support rather than practitioners or community organizations (Rominov, Giallo, Pilkington, & Whelan, 2018; Smith et al., 2015). Perception of support is very important to a father's involvement in his infant's care (Castillo & Fenzi-Crossman, 2010).

In health care settings, fathers often feel ignored on postpartum units and at well-baby visits; frequently, practitioners direct their questions and attention to the mother of the infants (De Montigny, Lacharite, & Devault, 2012; Garfield & Isacco, 2006; Ellberg, Hogberg, & Lindh, 2010). This inattention to the fathers' needs can be attributed to the US health care system, which is not set up to deliver services to fathers during the perinatal and infancy time periods (Carlson et al., 2014). Practitioners must remember that fathers are parents, too, with similar role transitions and parenting educational needs as mothers (Dallas, 2009). Ultimately, practitioners are uniquely positioned to promote the fathers' parenting skills (Aqil et al., 2019; Benzies, Magill-Evans, Harrison, MacPhail, & Kimak, 2008) and offer support to fathers as they assume the paternal role (De Montigny & Lacharite, 2004; Tiedje & Darling-Fisher, 2003). It is important that practitioners engage fathers in the care of their children by shifting their expectations of fathers in the parenting role (Yogman & Garfield, 2016).

Community organizations provide resources and services to fathers in the community. However, some fathers may not access these resources for a variety of reasons, including the following: (1) well-baby visits are offered at inconvenient times for fathers (Garfield & Isacco, 2006), (2) fathers may have traditional masculinity beliefs and prefer to manage their own problems without outside assistance (Hoy, 2012; McKenzie, Jenkin, Gabrielle, & Collins, 2016), and (3) fathers may be too depressed or stressed to reach out for assistance (Kendrick, Anderson, & Moore, 2007). Typically, father-focused community programs offer a variety of outcomes such as work training opportunities and employment assistance, responsible fatherhood education, healthy couple relationship communication and co-parenting education, assessment of mental health problems, and reduction of risky and criminal behaviors with the goal of empowering the father to confidently take care of his infant (Bronte-Tinkew, Burkhauser, & Metz, 2012). Further, there is a need for organizations to provide programs and services to fathers during the prenatal period to facilitate their transition to the father role. Examples of services include preconception and reproductive care, physical and mental health services, and helping fathers understand their importance on the health of mothers and infants (Garfield & Isacco, 2006). Most importantly, service organizations and parenting programs must deliver equitable support to fathers from a cultural context (Panter-Brick et al., 2014). Community organizations and programs must use evidenced-based strategies to promote father involvement in maternal and child health (Davis et al., 2016; National Academics of Sciences, Engineering, & Medicine, 2016).

Practice

The Study Description

The purpose of this study was to describe how social networks, health care practitioners, and community organizations provide social support to first-time and experienced fathers during the first year after birth of their infants. After review and approval from a university internal review board, 35 low-income fathers were interviewed for this descriptive, qualitative study within 2–12 months after the birth of their child. Inclusion criteria included the following: (1) being 18 years or older, (2) delivery of a full term, healthy infant, and (3) able to read and speak English. Most fathers were African American (91%), experienced fathers (60%), and single (71%) and reported basic high school education or equivalent (77%) and low annual incomes of less than $20,000 (80%). The mean age of the fathers was 31 years (SD = 5). Semi-structured interviews were used to collect data and structured content analysis (Hsieh & Shannon, 2005) was used to analyze the data (Hsieh & Shannon, 2005).

For this study, the researchers partnered with the community organizations, Compassion Outreach of America (COA), Head Start, and Bureau of Family Health to assist with father recruitment. COA is a nonprofit organization that was founded in 2008 to create a safe, thriving community for children in the St. Claude area and surrounding neighborhoods, which are inner city areas in New Orleans, Louisiana. The mission of COA is to reduce homicide through education and promote community development in these neighborhoods. Currently, COA provides monthly support groups for fathers and attends father events in the New Orleans community. During the data collection period, the founding director of COA completed the interviews and came to the project with previous experience with conducting community interviews and focus groups. The executive director managed the recruitment process.

Description of Fathers Living in the St. Claude Area of New Orleans, Louisiana

Most of the fathers in this study resided in the St. Claude neighborhood, in the district commonly called the Bywater district. The population for this neighborhood consists of 5,771 people and 2,630 households (Statistical Atlas, 2018). Most of the residents who live in this area are African American (81.9%), are single (62%), and have a high school diploma (44.9%). Employment among males between 25 to 64 years old is 51.6%, and males are primarily employed in lower paying occupations such as food service, clerical administrative, sales, facilities, construction, transportation, repair, and personal care. The median household income in this area is $22,900 a year, which means half of the residents make less than $22,000 per year and the other half makes more than $22,900 per year (Demographic Statistical Atlas of the United States [DSAUS], 2017). This median income is lower than the median income in New Orleans which is $36,999 per year (United States Census Bureau, 2017). Further, African American residents who live in the St. Claude neighborhood are more likely on food stamps (38.1%) compared to mixed races (13.8%) (DSAUS, 2017). There are many economic and living implications for African American residents in New Orleans since the poverty level is 34% (Talk Poverty, 2017). Residents living in the St. Claude neighborhood are at high risk for having economic difficulties and inequities in living conditions.

Case Studies

The following two case studies provide information on the four types of social support (emotional, instrumental, informational, and appraisal) and informal and formal networks that the fathers reported at the time of the interview. A new and experienced father case was used to describe their social support needs. All fathers were African American, were low-income, and had completed high school, and all infants were born full term without complications.

New Father (Ray–pseudonym)

Ray is 26 years old, married and living with his wife, and a first-time father of a baby girl. At the time of the interview, his baby was 12 months old, was bottle-fed in early infancy, and was born by vaginal delivery. Ray is employed part-time and reports an income of less than $10,000 per year. Ray and his wife have been in a relationship for eight years and he accompanied his wife on prenatal visits but did not attend the delivery. After the baby was born, he was involved with many activities such as feeding, changing diapers, talking to his baby, putting his baby to bed, and spending time with the baby. In addition, Ray states he has a lot of previous experience taking care of other children while growing up.

Ray's social network consisted of a lot of people who helped him learn how to take care of his family. The following quote expresses this sentiment:

A lot of people have stepped up and really, you know what I'm saying, not only gave us motivation, but gave us, you know what I'm saying, the foundation, the blueprint, you know. All you got to do is alter our steps … and they gave us the blueprint of what to do. How to take care of our families and what to do to be there for our families.

[informational and appraisal support]

In regard to the role of health care practitioners (HCPs) (nurses and physicians), Ray stated he needed more attention and direction from the HCPs on the postpartum unit. He stated "Man, as far as the nurses, you know, is all into the woman … you ask yourself, "What can I do to help?" or "Can I hold her right now?" Also, Ray stated the doctor did not tell him that he could hold and feed the baby either. Further, Ray verbalized the importance of fathers as a parent in the following quote: "You think it's all about the mom … but this is my baby, you know, she came from me." In regard to treatment in hospitals, Ray stated:

It's just that we play the back burner when it comes to hospitals and when it comes to our family, really foremost our Black families, they see Black families and ignore the Black male. It's as if we temporary or something.

[racism and lack of support]

In regard to other places in the community that he could access support, Ray stated, "There ain't too many resources for a Black man like that …. Really, to tell you the truth, if we want these things, we have to create them in the family." Overall, Ray verbalized satisfaction with the social support given by his family and social network but needed more guidance with infant care and acknowledgment from HCPs on his role as father of his baby. Finally, Ray was not satisfied with the support from his formal network.

Experienced Father (Daniel–pseudonym)

Daniel is 25 years old, single and living with the mother of his baby, is an experienced father of a boy baby, and has two other children. At the time of the interview, his baby was five months old, bottle-fed, and born by cesarean section. Daniel is employed full-time and reports an income of less than $20,000 per year. Daniel and the mother of his baby have been in a relationship for seven years and he was at delivery when his baby was born. In addition, Daniel was very involved in activities during the pregnancy with the mother of the baby such as attending prenatal classes and prenatal visits, financially supporting the mother, and providing emotional support. After the baby was born, he was involved with many activities such as feeding, changing diapers, talking to his baby, putting his baby to bed, and spending time and playing with the baby. Also, Daniel indicates he has a lot of experience taking care of other children before he had his children.

Daniel's social support network consists of his grandmother, the mother of his baby, his mom, and her mom and dad. He states he has called his grandmother with questions related to the baby's illness and that his social network provides them with whatever they need. The following quote describes the assistance he receives from his social network:

> It's really our household. Me and my girl work together to keep everything stable .... If [we need] a case of water, they'll [referring to his social network] just come through ... and give us some water. So that's like the people who I go to—it's not really like cousins and friends, it's my grandmother, my mom, my dad, her mom, or her dad .... Everybody like, they really in tune with us.
> [emotional and instrumental support]

In regard to HCPs, Daniel states the physician and hospital should have been more "proactive" and provided him with tips for taking care of his child. He states:

> They could have at least told me something ... or mailed me something and be like, since you came to the hospital for this [meaning birth of infant], I'm going to refresh your memory on something that I told you if you might have forgot. You know what I'm saying, that'd be easier.
> [lack of informational support]

In regard to community organizations and resources, Daniel stated he did not use any daycare for his children. He states, "I ain't into daycares. I always watch my kids myself and if not, then my girl or the people I named help us out." However, when asked about a place in the community where he can get support, Daniel stated he went to a barbershop for support. He states:

> ... I just found one barber and stuck to him, but when I go its always positive talk, peaceful talk, he [the barber] used to be a preacher so, yea, he like a father figure.
> [emotional support]

Overall, Daniel's informal social network was made up of close kinships but, interestingly, cousins and friends were not included in the social network. In regard to support from HCPs and hospitals, Daniel expressed a need for more teaching on infant care and educational products that helped him refresh his understanding of infant care. In regard to access and use of community organizations, Daniel stated he did not use daycares but instead relied on his household and kinship to help take care of his new baby. However, he stated he spent a lot of time at a particular barbershop for "peaceful talk."

Lessons Learned

The Recruitment Process

This work was funded for two years and after the first year, several adjustments were made in the data collection process. During the first year, an African American father facilitator was hired to recruit and interview fathers for the study. Flyers were distributed at local clinics, community organizations, and daycare centers, and a dedicated phone was available for fathers to call in and leave their contact information if they were interested in participating in the study. Even though we had partnered with many community organizations, medical clinics, and a hospital, we had only recruited five fathers to the study at the end of the first year. After talking with my program officer at an annual visit, a suggestion was made to change my partnership plan to a collaborative relationship so that the community organization could recruit fathers for the study. The program officer provided three organizations for the primary investigator to consider. After meeting with the COA executive director, a collaborative relationship was formed on recruiting and interviewing fathers using a memorandum of understanding agreement. At the conclusion of the second year, 25 fathers had been recruited and interviewed for the study. The lessons learned in this study include the following:

- Partner with an organization who is interested in your project, who has deep connections and social networks in the community, and who has a vested interest in your project.
- Partner with an organization that can provide direct referrals or recruitments to the study. Establishing a formal contract with organizations is a good option for delineating responsibilities and financially compensating for their time and services.
- Recruiting participants by only posting flyers is difficult in obtaining an adequate sample. Organizational representatives must take an active role in recruiting participants to the study.
- Interviewers must be culturally sensitive and able to relate to the needs and experiences of the sample population.

The Study Findings

The purpose of this descriptive, qualitative study was to determine the social support needs of low-income, African American fathers in early parenthood and identify the types of support fathers receive from family and friends, HCPs, and community organizations. The study findings present a picture of 35 low-income, new and experienced fathers living in an urban setting and the support they received in transitioning to their father role. The study findings show that fathers commonly receive more parenting information and support from their family members rather than HCPs and community organizations. In addition, fathers appreciate the emotional, instrumental, and informational support they receive from their inner circle (most often the baby's mother, his mother, grandmother, and sister) and receiving advice from others and observing interactions of other fathers assisted them in appraising or evaluating his role as a father. Also, fathers were very selective about whom they asked for help, meaning some fathers did not ask help from their friends or other family members.

Unfortunately, fathers often felt ignored by HCPs during the postpartum period and well-baby office visits. On the postpartum unit, some nurses focused their teaching and care on the mother and did not address the educational needs of the father. Further, nurses and doctors at well-baby visits did not involve the father in the baby's care and primarily asked questions of the baby's mother. In general, fathers wanted guidance and information on taking care of their baby, including information on infant feeding, the baby's crying and sleep patterns, how to detect signs and symptoms of illness in their baby, and when to call the doctor. In this study, HCPs provided mainly provided informational support.

Interestingly, most fathers could not identify a specific community organization that assisted them after the birth of their baby, but some fathers did access other resources such as churches for spiritual and nursery care, barbershops for conversations, and neighborhood social events in someone's home to promote family activities. In general, most fathers stated they needed more resources from community organizations including job training, parenting classes to improve infant skills, and financial assistance for paying for child supplies and transportation needs. Using these resources, fathers received emotional, instrumental, informational, and appraisal types of support. In summary, fathers used resources in their local communities but need more information and guidance on how to contact larger community organizations for assistance.

Therefore, fathers need better support as they transition to the father role. HCPs and community organizations must recognize that fathers are parents, too, and deserve fair and equitable care. Family and friends need to know the best way to support new fathers since they rely on the support of their kinship during their transition to the father role. The following recommendations support father-friendly practices:

- Develop more comprehensive, early care programs that are easily accessible to urban neighborhoods. Offer infant caregiving information to fathers that will enhance their skills, confidence, and transition to the father role.

- During postpartum and well-child visits, involve the father with all parent education and child decisions, using directed and focused communication.
- Community organizations should strengthen the capacity of fathers to father by offering programs that (1) strengthen fathers' infant caretaking skills, (2) provide financial assistance with infant caretaking supplies and transportation needs, and (3) improve economic and parenting opportunities for fathers by offering job training and parenting resources.

Conclusion

The process of becoming a father is multifactorial and dynamic as fathers become actively involved in taking care of their infants. Little research has been conducted on the social support needs of first-time and experienced fathers as they transition to the father role, especially in ethnic groups. There is an urgent need to determine the type of support that is needed by African American fathers with infants living in an urban setting. Given the different household structures of fathers in the study and the fact that most of the fathers were experienced fathers, it is important to determine social support needs of fathers with infants and not assume that experienced fathers have less social support needs.

Using the approach, "it takes a village to raise a child," fathers were asked about their social support needs from families and friends, health care professionals, and community organizations. Not surprising, fathers were primarily supported by their family members and as demonstrated in the two case studies, received the following four types of support: emotional, instrumental, informational, and appraisal support. However, some fathers reported they felt ignored by health care providers on postpartum units and at well-child visits and that HCPs primarily focused on the parenting needs of mothers. In regard to community organizations, the majority of fathers could not name a community organization that they used after the birth of their infant; instead, fathers stated they used local groups such as churches, barbershops, and neighborhood events as a source of support. More research is needed on the social support needs of fathers in urban settings to determine how community organizations and HCPs can provide better father-friendly practices to support fathers as they transition to the father role.

References

Alio, A.P., Lewis, C.A., Scarborough, K., Harries, K., & Fiscella, K. (2013). A community perspective on the role of fathers during pregnancy: A qualitative study. *BMC Pregnancy & Childbirth*, 13(60), 1–17.

Aqil, A., Allport, B.S., Johnson, S.B., Nelson, T., Labrique, A.B., & Marcell, A.V. (2019). Content to share with expectant fathers: Views of professionals focused on father involvement. *Midwifery*, 70, 119–126.

Asenhed, L., Kilstam, J., Alehagen, S., & Baggens, C. (2013). Becoming a father is an emotional roller coaster-An analysis of first-time fathers' blogs. *Journal of Clinical Nursing*, 23, 1309–1317.

Association of Maternal & Child Programs. (2009). *AMCHP fact sheet: Father involvement in MCH programs*. Retrieved from http://www.amchp.org/programsandtopics/womens-health/resources/Documents/Father-Involvement-Fact-Sheet.pdf.

Benzies, K., Magill-Evans, J., Harrison, M.J., MacPhail, S., & Kimak, C. (2008). Strengthening new fathers' skills in interaction with their 5-month-old infants: Who benefits from a brief intervention? *Public Health Nursing*, 25(5), 431–439.

Bond, M.J. (2010). The missing link in MCH: Paternal involvement in pregnancy outcomes. *American Journal of Men's Health*, 4(4), 285–286.

Bronte-Tinkew, J., Burkhauser, M., & Metz, A.J.R. (2012). Elements of promising practices in fatherhood programs: Evidence-based research findings on interventions for father. *Fathering*, 10(1), 6–30.

Bronte-Tinkew, J., Carrano, J., Horowitz, A., & Kinkawa, A. (2008). Involvement among nonresident fathers and links to infant cognitive outcomes. *Journal of Family Issues*, 29(9), 1211–1244.

Carlson, J., Edleson, J.L., & Kimball, E. (2014). First-time fathers' experiences of and desires for formal support: A multiple lens perspective. *Fathering*, 12(3), 242–261.

Castillo, J.T., & Fenzi-Crossman, A. (2010). The relationship between non-marital fathers' social networks and social capital and father involvement. *Child and Family Social Work*, 15, 66–76.

Commission on Paternal Involvement in Pregnancy Outcomes. (2009). *Best and promising practices for improving research, policy and practice on paternal involvement in pregnancy outcomes*.Joint Center for Political and Economic Studies. Retrieved from http://www.nationalhealthystart.org/site/assets/docs/CPIPO%20Report%20051910%20Final.pdf.

Dallas, C.M. (2009). Interactions between adolescent fathers and health care professionals during pregnancy, labor, and early postpartum. *Journal of Obstetric, Gynecologic, and Neonatal Nursing*, 38, 290–299.

Davis, J., Vyankandondera, J., Luchters, S., Simon, D., & Holmes, W. (2016). Male involvement in reproductive, maternal and child health: A qualitative study of policy maker and practitioner perspectives in the Pacific. *Reproductive Health*, 13(81), 1–11.

Dayton, C.J., Buczkowski, R., Muzik, M., Hicks, L., Walsh, T.B., & Boeknek, E.L. (2016). Expectant fathers' beliefs and expectations about fathering as they prepare to parent a new infant. *Social Work Research*, 40(4), 225–236.

De Montigny, F., & Lacharite, C. (2004). Fathers' perceptions of the immediate postpartal period. *Journal of Obstetric, Gynecologic, and Neonatal Nursing*, 33, 328–339.

De Montigny, F., Lacharite, C., & Devault, A. (2012). Transition to fatherhood: Modeling the experience of fathers of breastfed infants. *Advances in Nursing Science*, 35(3), e11–e22.

Ellberg, L., Hogberg, U., & Lindh, V. (2010). "We feel like one, they see us as two": New parents' discontent with postnatal care. *Midwifery*, 26, 463–468.

Gadsden, V.L., Ford, M., & Breiner, H. (2016). *Parenting matters: Supporting parents of children ages* (pp. 0–8). The National Academies Press. Retrieved from http://nap.edu/21868.

Garfield, C.F., & Isacco, A. (2006). Fathers and the well-child visit. *Pediatrics*, 117, e637–e645.

Giallo, R., Brown, S., Kingston, D., Wade, C., Cooklin, A., & Christensen Nicholson, J.M. (2015). Trajectories of fathers' psychological distress across the early parenting period: Implications for parenting. *Journal of Family Psychology*, 5, 766–776.

Henshaw, E.J., Cooper, M.A., Jaramillo, M., Lamp, J.M., Jones, A.L., & Wood, T. (2018). "Trying to figure out if you're doing things right, and where to get the info:" Parents recall information and support needed during the first 6 weeks postpartum. *Maternal and Child Health Journal*, 22, 1668–1675.

Healthy People. (2020). *Maternal, infant, and child health.* Retrieved from http://www. healthypeople.gov/2020/leading-health-indicators/2020-lhi-topics.

Hoy, S. (2012). Beyond men behaving badly: A meta-ethnography of men's perspectives on psychological distress and help seeking. *International Journal of Men's Health*, 1193, 202–226.

House, J.S. (1981). *Work stress and social support.* Reading, MA: Addison-Wesley.

Hsieh, H.F., & Shannon, S.E. (2005). Three approaches to qualitative content analysis. *Qualitative Health Research*, 15(9), 1277–1288.

Kendrick, L., Anderson, N.L.R., & Moore, B. (2007). Perceptions of depression among young African American Men. *Family & Community Health*, 30(1), 63–73.

Kim, M., Kang, S.K., Yee, B., Shim, S.Y., & Chung, M. (2016). Paternal involvement and early infant neurodevelopment: The mediation roles of maternal parenting stress. *BMC Pediatrics*, 16(212), 1–8.

Lamb, M.E. (2010). *The role of the father in child development* (5th ed.). Hoboken, New Jersey: John Wiley & Sons.

Lu, M.C., Jones, J., Bond, M.J., Wright, K., Pampuang, M., Maidenberg, M., & Rowley, D.L. (2010). Where is the F in MCH? Father involvement in African American families. *Ethnicity & Disease*, 20, S2–49-S2-61.

Martin, C.R., & Redshaw, M. (2010). Fathers in the twenty-first century: Essential role or accessory? *Journal of Reproductive and Infant Psychology*, 28(2), 113–115.

Maternal and Child Health Bureau. (2020). *Building healthy communities.* Health Resources & Services Administration. Retrieved from https://mchb.hrsa.gov/about.

McKenzie, S., Jenkin, G., & Collings, S. (2016). Men's perspective of common mental health problems: A metasynthesis of qualitative research. *International Journal of Men's Health*, 15(1), 80–104.

Murphy, A.D., Gordon, D., Sherrod, H., Dancy, V., & Kershaw, T. (2012). Friends, family, and foes: The influence of fathers' social networks. *American Journal of Men's Health*, 7(3), 228–242.

National Academics of Sciences, Engineering, & Medicine. (2016). *Parenting matters: Supporting parents of children 0–8.* Retrieved from https://www.nap.edu/resource/21868/ RiB_parenting_matters.pdf.

National Healthy Start Association. (2015). *Male involvement: Where dads matter.* Retrieved from http://www.amchp.org/programsandtopics/womens-health/resources/Documents/ Father-Involvement-Fact-Sheet.pdf.

Panter-Brick, C., Burgess, A., Eggerman, M., McAllister, F., Pruett, K., & Leckman, J.F. (2014). Practitioner review: Engaging fathers-Recommendation for a game change in parenting interventions based on a systematic review. *Journal of Child Psychology and Psychiatry*, 55(11), 1187–1212.

Rominov, H., Giallo, R., Pilkington, P.D., & Whelan, T.A. (2018). "Getting help for yourself is a helping your baby": Fathers' experiences of support for a mental health and parenting in the perinatal period. *Psychology of Men & Masculinity*, 19(3), 457–468.

Seymour, M., Dunning, M., Cooklin, A., & Giallo, R. (2014). Socioecological factors associated with father's well-being difficulties in the early parenting period. *Clinical Psychologist*, 18, 63–73.

Smith, T.K., Tandon, S.D., Blair-Merritt, M.H., & Hanson, J.L. (2015). Parenting needs of urban, African American fathers. *American Journal of Men's Health*, *9*(4), 317–331.

Statistical Atlas. (2018). Retrieved from https://statisticalatlas.com/neighborhood/ Louisiana/New-Orleans/St-Claude/Overview#top.

Talk Poverty. (2017). *Louisiana report-2017-Talk poverty*. Retrieved from https:// talkpoverty.org/state-year-report/louisiana-2017-report/.

Tiedje, L.B., & Darling-Fisher, C. (2003). Promoting father-friendly practices. *MCN: The American Journal of Maternal Child Nursing*, 28(6), 350–359.

Tokki, M., Comrie-Thomson, L., Davis, J., Portela, A., Chersich, M., & Luchters, S. (2018). *Involving men to improve maternal and newborn health: A systematic review of the effectiveness of interventions*. PLOS One, 13(1), 1–16.

Towe-Goodman, N.R., Willoughby, M., Gustafsson, H.C., Mills-Koonce, W.R., Cox, M.J., & Blair, C. (2014). Fathers' sensitive parenting and the development of early executive functioning. *Journal of Family Psychology*, 28(60), 867–876.

United States Census Bureau. (2017). *Median household income in New Orleans city, Louisiana*. Retrieved from https://data.census.gov/cedsci/all?q=%202017%20New%20Orleans %20median%20household%20income&g=1600000US2255000&tid=ACSST1Y2017.S1 901&t=Income%20%28Households,%20Families,%20Individuals%29%3AHousehold %20and%20Family&y=2017&vintage=2017&layer=VT_2017_160_00_PY_D1&cid= S1901_C01_001E.

Yogman, M., & Garfield, C.F. (2016). Fathers' roles in the care and development of their children: The role of pediatricians. *American Academy of Pediatrics*, 138(1), e1–e15.

3 Engaging and Working with Fathers Toward Workforce Readiness

What About the Men?

Angelia D. O'Neal

Introduction—What About the Men?

Life skills. Soft skills. Limited community resources. Negative images. Education and racial disparities. To begin to address these larger problems, it is necessary to ask some basic questions: Why do so few African American men graduate from high school? Why is the employment rate of African American men, both in youth and during their prime working years, so low (Cherry, 2020)? African American men face growing employment problems. Between 2000 and 2014, the employment rate for African American men aged 25 to 34 declined from 81.9% to 71.3%. While the White male employment rate also declined over this period, the decline in the African American male rate was greater and significantly so. The racial employment rate gap among these prime, working-age men rose from 9.8% to 13.9%, an increase of more than 40%. The teen employment rate for African American men fell from 28.9% to 16.4%, also a larger percentage decline than for White teenagers. What explains these growing racial disparities? Studies have consistently found that, when job applicants are plentiful, employers are much more reluctant to hire African American workers. Often, all applicants with criminal records, those who live in high-crime areas, and those who cannot provide reliable personal recommendations are immediately screened out and do not make it to the interview stage. This screening process especially hurts African American men (Cherry, 2020).

Further employment analysis for African American males, young and old, has shown the fact that they do not have sustainable jobs. Tsoi-A-Fatt (2020) states "regardless of educational level or past work history, African American males are less likely to be working than any other demographic in the United States" (p. 17). Some have limited employment options because they lack postsecondary degrees or additional training necessary for higher level jobs. Yet regardless of how much training they may have, African American males are less likely to get a job interview simply because they have a name like "DeAndre" instead of "Andrew." African American males between ages 16 to 24 fare the worst, the ages that often establish a person's earning trajectory for a lifetime.

In 2010, 17.4% of African American men over age 20 were unemployed, almost double the rate of White men (U.S. Bureau of Labor Statistics, 2010). In low-income communities of color, the percentage is often even higher. Unemployment and underemployment in communities of color has been an issue for several decades. African American men who have jobs are often underemployed. Many African American men have jobs that pay wages not sufficient to support themselves or their families, and they also lack benefits such as paid sick leave and health insurance. Among African Americans who have a bachelor's degree, only 43% have "good" jobs where they make at least $14.51 per hour and receive health insurance and a pension. Across all education levels, only about one in five African Americans has a "good" job. The current economic downturn has had a catastrophic effect on job prospects and overall financial stability for everyone, particularly African American men (Tsoi-A-Fatt, 2010).

Incarceration

Young men of color with prior involvement in the criminal legal system face acute difficulty in obtaining employment that stems from their criminal record and their race. In a study of over 3,000 employers in four metropolitan areas, nearly 20% reported they would "definitely not" hire an applicant with a criminal record, and 42% indicated they would "probably not" do so (Flake, 2015).

Discrimination against people with criminal legal system involvement magnifies persistently high hiring discrimination against people of color, particularly those who are African American and Latinx (Quillian, Pager, Hexel, & Midtbøen, 2017). In effect, even after young men of color have served their time, they continue to be punished. In recent years, states and cities have recognized such barriers and passed legislation intended to increase the chances of employment for people who have been involved in the criminal legal system.

Fourteen states and dozens of cities have enacted laws that limit discrimination against people with a criminal record in public employment, and five of those states have extended the checks to the private sector (Flake, 2015). The most popular version of this type of reform is "ban-the-box" laws, which remove the conviction history question from job applications and delay background checks until later in the hiring process. Though several states were early adopters, President Obama's 2015 endorsement of the policies triggered their expansion. Thirty-five states have now passed "ban-the-box" laws (Avery & Hernandez, 2019). Despite some research that ban-the-box policies reduce the likelihood of employers calling back or hiring African American and Latinx men without criminal records, recent research focusing on public employment disputes those findings and shows that the laws generally raise the probability of employment for those with convictions (Doleac & Hansen, 2017).

Educational Attainment

Terrible schools, absent parents, racism, the decline in blue collar jobs, and a subculture that glorifies swagger over work are all causes of the worsening statistics about African American males. We have known that African Americans are not making economic progress. A recent report from the Economic Policy Institute (EPI), a left-leaning think tank, shows that the African American–White wage gap is now the widest it has been since 1979. What is more interesting, though, is how inequality has been increasing, and for whom. It used to be that low-skilled African American workers suffered the greatest disadvantage relative to their White counterparts. But there has been a strange reversal in the past 40 years. EPI finds that the African American–White wage gap has become wider – and is widening faster – among those with more education. In 1980, African American men entering the job market with just a high school diploma earned 15% less than similar White men on average. In contrast, African American men with bachelor's degrees or more earned only 5% less than similar White male college graduates.

College, in other words, once seemed a surefire route to something approaching racial equity. Nowadays, the picture is more complicated. While the racial wage gap among less-educated men has held steady at about 15%, that gap for men with college diplomas increased significantly in the 1980s, and now hovers between 15% and 20%. In 2014, the penalty for being educated-while-African American was about 18%. The penalty for less-educated African American men was 16% (Guo, 2016).

Public Policy

Another factor is related to an otherwise successful policy: the stricter enforcement of child support. Improved collection of money from absent fathers has been a pillar of welfare system overhaul. But the system can leave young men feeling overwhelmed with debt and deter them from seeking legal work since a large share of any earnings could be seized. About half of all African American men in their late 20s and early 30s who did not go to college are noncustodial fathers (Holzer, Offner, & Edelman, 2006).

Recent studies identified a range of government programs and experiments, especially education and training efforts like the Job Corps, that had shown success and could be scaled up. Scholars call for intensive new efforts to give children a better start, including support for parents and extra schooling for children. They call for teaching skills to prisoners and helping them reenter society more productively and for less automatic incarceration of minor offenders. In a society where higher education is vital to economic success, Mincy (Eckholm, 2006) said programs to help more men enter and succeed in college may hold promise. But he lamented the dearth of policies and resources to aid single men. "We spent $50 billion in efforts that produced the turnaround for poor women…. We are not even beginning to think about the men's problem on similar orders of magnitude. There's something very different happening with young African American men, and it's something we can no longer ignore .... Over the last two decades, the economy did great and low-skilled women, helped by public policy, latched onto it. But young African American men were falling farther back" (Eckholm, 2006). Eckholm (2006) stated, "African American men in the United States face a far direr situation than is portrayed by common employment and education statistics, a flurry of new scholarly studies warned, and it has worsened in recent years even as an economic boom and a welfare overhaul have brought gains to African American women and other groups."

Although African American fathers continued to struggle with overcoming hurdles to self-sufficiency in the workplace, Corey S. Sutton, former chairman and employment readiness trainer for M.E.N.S. Wear, Inc. stated,

> employment of the African American male is a multi-faceted issue and dilemma for the African American community and America. The root cause can be traced back for generations to our ancestors and how the African American male was viewed in America. From our initial enslavement the African American male has only been viewed a manual laborer with little to no skills. Fast forward to today, and we can say there has been some advancement, moderate at best, in that attitude but not enough to effectively include the African American male as a viable contributor to economic growth and development of our society. The moderate advances have primarily happened in the Arts and Entertainment fields and most recently in Politics and Scholastic arenas.

Sutton further stated, "the core of American and business economic engine lies in the skilled and semi-skilled individual." African American fathers have faced several obstacles to obtain the tools necessary to be "successful." These obstacles range from social, economic, cultural, and geographical influences. The parenthesis around "successful" is there for a reason. Society has hijacked what that looks like and in particular in the African American community. As I worked with various groups of males, it was amazing to see how they viewed themselves, and what their success looked like in the workplace, when compared to society.

Recent studies show that as time moves forward, several of the concerns that plagued African American males in the past are still prevalent today. Besides contributing to a negative civic environment, stereotypes of African American fathers matter because they may demoralize support for efforts to reduce racial disparities. If White people view African Americans as lazy, they are less likely to support government anti-poverty programs. Or if it is commonly believed that African American people are unintelligent or violent, it will hinder efforts for school or neighborhood integration, for example. And if African American people believe these negative things about their own group, it may contribute to low self-esteem and other problems.

Issues of race and policy are understood by most White Americans as being about individuals and relationships, not systems and structures, and that means the explanation for gaps in achievement are often understood as resulting from personal successes or failures rather than external influences. Therefore, even if people recognize that disparities exist, they often blame disparities on individual failures alone, not systemic influences. Furthermore, if people fail to recognize that discrimination exists, many will continue to think it is solely due to personal prejudice and do not see the influence of institutional racism. Overcoming this dynamic will be a central challenge for those who seek policy solutions.

But would more accurate knowledge help or hurt efforts to address disparities? If people had more accurate knowledge of the disparities that exist, would it inspire them to address them? Or would it just feed negative stereotypes? The answer to this question depends in large part on people's reasoning for why disparities exist. Even if there is widespread agreement that there are inequities between White and African American Americans, there is a fundamental disagreement about the cause of inequities.

Practice—Making Employment the Next Step

Founded in 2004, M.E.N.S. (i.e., Making Employment the Next Step) Wear, Inc. established its roots in Georgia to address the need for workforce readiness skill development for African American males, with a special attention to fathers. As the founder of the agency, I have a strong background in management and career services and a natural love for the appreciation of professionalism to include professional dress. My experience in this area prepared me to enjoy helping people in acquiring success in career readiness. I understood that job readiness (skill development; both soft and hard, education, and professional imaging—now referred to as branding) were crucial elements to obtaining and hopefully securing a "good" job that could turn into a sustainable career. On the contrary, coming from the for-profit world, my plans were not to open a nonprofit organization. The plan was to establish a professional personal wardrobe service agency to help the thousands of professional males in Atlanta with maintaining a professional business image at all times. However, the more I planned the business – researching and writing a business plan to provide GREAT services to my target market, African American males – research revealed something completely different from what I was seeing daily around the metropolitan Atlanta area: professional businessmen in three-piece suits driving luxury cars and taking care of business! On the surface, two out of three African American males seen on a daily basis appeared to be very successful. However, I was in for a rude awakening. Research on African American males in Atlanta, Georgia; Detroit, Michigan (my home state); and in many major cities in America spoke primarily on the plight of African American males.

My husband and father of our four-year-old son, at that time, was a college graduate with a bachelor's degree in criminal justice and African American studies. For months, he searched for jobs and applied to jobs but could not find anything. To my surprise, this plight was beginning to show itself in more poignant ways for African American males. It began to weigh him down emotionally and spiritually and diminish his self-esteem as a father and husband. Then one day he said, "You know what? You ladies have it made. There are all sorts of resources available for you. I wish we [African American males] had a central place that we could go to find resources, help us with the job search process, or just a place where I could go as a man, and a father to get support." Call it an epiphany, but the light came on when a small voice within said, "What about men that cannot afford your professional wardrobe service? What are they going to do?" Thus, M.E.N.S. Wear, Inc. was born—an agency designed to be the brother agency to Dress for Success for women, a resource and training center for males.

Since 2004, the agency has provided training and/or services to over 1,200 at-risk adult and young adult males in the metropolitan Atlanta area. M.E.N.S. Wear, Inc.'s target population is underrepresented men aged 18–49 years old. However, services and training are provided to custodial and noncustodial fathers, middle and high school male students, and individuals in general who have been unsuccessful at securing employment. One of them told a story so commonplace it hardly bears notice here. He quit school in the tenth grade to sell drugs; fathered four children with three mothers; and spent several stretches in jail for drug possession, parole violations, and other crimes. "I was with the street life, but now I feel like I"ve got to get myself together," he said recently in the row-house flat he shares with his girlfriend and four children. "You get tired of incarceration." He is 28, planning to look for work, perhaps as a mover, and he noted optimistically that he had not been locked up in six months.

A group of men, including this young man, gathered at the Center for Fathers, Families and Workforce Development, one of several private agencies working to help men strengthen their character along with workplace skills. The clients readily admit to their own bad choices but say they also fight a pervasive sense of hopelessness. "It hurts to get that boot in the face all the time," said a 34-year-old participant. "I've had a lot of charges but only a few convictions," he said of his criminal record. He is now trying to strike out on his own, developing a party space for rentals, but he needs help with business skills. "I don't understand," said a 47-year-old participant, "if a man wants to change, why won't society give him a chance to prove he's a changed person?" He has a lot of records to overcome, he admits, including his recent 15-year stay in the state penitentiary for armed robbery. He led a visitor down the Pennsylvania Avenue strip he wants to escape – past idlers, addicts, and hustlers; storefront churches; and fortress-like liquor stores – and described a life that seemed inevitable. He sold marijuana for his parents, he said, left school in the sixth grade, and later dealt heroin and cocaine. He was for decades addicted to heroin, he said, easily keeping the habit during three terms in prison. But during his last long stay, he also studied hard to get a G.E.D. and an associate's degree. Now out for 18 months, he is living in a home for recovering drug addicts. He is working a $10-an-hour warehouse job while he ponders how to make a living from his real passion, drawing and graphic arts. "I don't want to be a criminal at 50," he said.

Bridging Business and the Community

Understanding the diverse needs of African American fathers, M.E.N.S. Wear, Inc partnered with government agencies, educational institutions, private businesses, and nongovernmental organizations. The agency provides personal/social adjustment training and professional wardrobe clothing to "bridge the gap" in workforce development. True to its mission, the goal of M.E.N.S. Wear, Inc. is to empower individuals with becoming (1) confident, positive employees; (2) pioneers in building stronger communities; and (3) major contributors to the US economy. In 2015, M.E.N.S. Wear, Inc. launched a social enterprise venture that established how nonprofit agencies could "rethink" operations by incorporating common business strategies to create self-sustaining social enterprises while achieving their mission. Since M.E.N.S. Wear, Inc. collected donated professional men clothing items and accessories, these items were primarily used for programming needs to service clients. Many (if not all) of the clients that received services needed professional attire to just begin looking for employment. Operating as a social enterprise, a portion of M.E.N.S. Wear, Inc.'s donations is sold to generate revenue to support operational and programming expenses. In 2016, M.E.N.S. Wear, Inc. collaborated with the National Retail Federation Foundation. M.E.N.S. Wear, Inc. established a unique training program, RetailWork$™, to help positively build the retail and service industries' next generation of talent: first-time job seekers and entry-level employees. The mission of RetailWork$™ enhanced the employability and customer service skills of youth and young adult males (and females) for lasting careers in customer service, retail, fashion, and management. The training modules offered through RetailWork$™ include the following:

- Customer service
- Retail industry fundamentals and inventory management
- Personal branding and professional business wardrobe building

The content is foundational and covers specific topics but also soft skills such as communication, teamwork, problem solving, etc. The program was launched in an inner-city mall in the heart of Atlanta, Georgia. The concept was great. Once the community learned that a nonprofit agency was in "their community" training young men and helping them develop soft and hard skills, it was well received. M.E.N.S. Wear, Inc. was even featured on a local news station for its ingenuity. The community shopped regularly, and word began to spread. However, anyone in the nonprofit arena knows that funding and revenue generation can be a long p-r-o-c-e-s-s and after reoccurring slow rent payments, the mall management office decided to rescind on its agreement. What a tragedy. The positive PR and impact that was being made in this inner-city mall was shut down because the "accountability system" was broken. Local customers regarded the mall as not only "taking money from consumer sales" but also as "giving back" and helping build their community. Needless to say, to this date, no other merchant had been placed in the vacated space.

Case Study

One collaboration that M.E.N.S. Wear, Inc. cherishes is with the Fulton County Teen Determined Active Dedicated Supportive (Teen DADS) initiative. The Teen DADs program emerged out of the historic "Call to Manhood Conference." The program provides comprehensive support services to young fathers to promote family stability through competent parenting skills, child health and welfare, financial and social stability, legal (legitimation), and healthy co-parenting relations. The overall goal is to strengthen families by providing young fathers with the skills, knowledge, and tools needed to provide appropriate care for their children's financial and emotional needs.

Over the years, M.E.N.S. Wear, Inc. provided life skills and soft skill development training workshops, professional interview clothing for job interviews, and other resources to support family reunification to empower the African American teen fathers through this program. QB, an alumni of the Fulton County Teen DADS program, successfully obtained a job with McDonalds and worked his way up to crew manager for the fast food restaurant. He was one of several young fathers who spoke to a group of 28 Teen DADS graduates and their families during a Teen DADS graduation ceremony. His goal was to obtain his GED to help him to provide for his daughters. After receiving his GED, he wants to attend Georgia Tech to become a mechanical or an electrical engineer.

Lessons Learned

As M.E.N.S. Wear, Inc. has learned, society and our culture have conditioned our men to work no matter what. Men understand that it is what one must do to support oneself and one's family. On the contrary,

M.E.N.S. Wear, Inc. has spent numerous of hours learning that African American males have not learned the value they have within themselves and really had not "learned of themselves." What skills and competencies have you acquired? It took time to educate them, including explaining what a "skill" versus a "competency" is. Once establishing an understanding of the two, we were able to progress with the steps to looking at job versus career, which most of these men thought were one in the same. As we went through the explanation to fathers, they begin to open up and understand their approach to employment and building a career.

"Most men learn this through family, friends and prior jobs," says Corey Sutton, former employment trainer of M.E.N.S. Wear, Inc. As we asked more questions, it became obvious that educating the fathers would need to include (1) personal accountability, (2) developing a skill set, (3) learning how to target a job to create skills for building a career, (4) employment search criteria, (5) resume building, (6) proper attire, (7) understanding the application process, (8) interview etiquette, (9) developing a personal plan to succeed, and (10) how to stay focused. A daunting list but it was workable because every African American male who M.E.N.S. Wear, Inc. worked with was willing and able to commit to the process. They saw the need and desired to improve their situation.

Conclusion

African American males are disadvantaged because communities receive less resources and services to support their needs. The communities remain unstable, and the people in the community remain impoverished. The time has come for solutions that break down employment disparities and instead create opportunities for skills training to prepare African American males for meaningful careers, harness the entrepreneurial spirit of African American males and transform it into successful business ventures, and build the wealth of African American families and communities. Mass unemployment is still an ongoing concern and breeding ground for trouble in African American communities. Lack of career-building opportunities sets an opportunity to create criminal activity and violence due to frustration and necessity, which eventual results in incarceration. Working firsthand with African American males as a whole has been an eye-opening experience. My analysis firmly concludes that this "uniquely designed" population needs strategic, unique, and holistic services and collaborations that create a platform to help them attain self-sufficiency. Experience has demonstrated that if private businesses, employers, nonprofit agencies, governmental agencies, and faith-based organizations can establish what I call an "*African-American Father Accountability System™*," males will feel that they have an authentic community support system that wants to lessen incarceration rates and support them as fathers, husbands, and employees. Like mothers, fathers need to believe they have resources and support. Like mothers, fathers want to provide the care and love that a child needs to succeed in school and in life. There is hope for African American males and the agencies that support them. As advocates, we must continue to fight and stand up for the rights, support system(s), and services for males and fathers. It is imperative that private businesses, non-governmental organizations, and other entities continue to develop collaborations that create needed services and resources for males.

References

Avery, B., & Hernandez, P. (2019). *Ban the box: US cities, counties, and states adopt fair hiring policies.* National Employment Law Project.

Cherry, R. (2020). Helping African American men thrive. *National Affairs,* 43. Retrieved from https://www.nationalaffairs.com/publications/detail/helping-African American-men-.

Doleac, J.L., & Hansen, B. (2017). Moving to job opportunities? The effect of "ban the box" on the composition of cities. *American Economic Review,* 107(5), 556–559.

Eckholm, E. (2006, March 20). Plight deepens for black men, studies warn. *The New York Times.*

Flake, D.F. (2015). When any sentence is a life sentence: Employment discrimination against ex-offenders. *Washington University Law Review,* 93(1), 45.

2018 Fulton County. (2018). Fulton County teen DADS program. Retrieved from http://www.fultoncountyga.gov/latest-news/7367-teen-father-aims-for-success.

Guo, J. (2016). *Why African American workers who do everything right still get left behind.* The Washington Post. Retrieved from http://www.washingtonpost.com/news/wonk/wp/2016/10/03/why-African American-workers-who-do-everything-right-still-get-left-behind/.

Holzer, H.J., Offner, P., & Edelman, P. (2006). *Reconnecting disadvantaged young men.* Urban Institute Press.

M.E.N.S. Wear, Inc. Retrieved from www.menswearinc.org.

Orfield, G. (2004). *Dropouts in America.* Harvard Education Press.

Quillian, L., Pager, D., Hexel, O., & Midtbøen, A.H. (2017). Meta-analysis of field experiments shows no change in racial discrimination in hiring over time. In *Proceedings of the National Academy of Sciences,* 114(41), 10870–10875.

Spievack, N., Brown, M., Durham, C., & Loprest, P. (2020). *Exploring approaches to increase economic opportunity for young men of color: A 10-year review.* Retrieved from http://bma.issuelab.org/resources/36412/36412.pdf.

2011 The Opportunity Agenda. (2011). *Perceptions of and by African American men.* Retrieved from https://opportunityagenda.org/.

Tsoi-A-Fatt, R. (2010). *We dream a world: The 2025 vision for African American men and boys.* Retrieved from https://www.opensocietyfoundations.org/publications/we-dream-world-2025-vision-black-men-and-boys.

U.S. Bureau of Labor Statistics (2010). *The employment situation.* Retrieved from https://bls.gov.

Wester, B.W. (2004). *Punishment and inequality in America.* Russell Sage Press.

4 Engaging and Working with African American Fathers Who are Alzheimer's Caregivers

Latrice Rollins and Gina Green-Harris

Introduction

In the United States, family caregivers are the backbone for the delivery of supportive services for individuals with a chronic, disabling, or serious health condition. They identify, arrange, and coordinate services and supports; provide emotional support; accompany their family member or friend to health provider visits; administer medications; assist with personal care (such as bathing and dressing); pay bills and deal with health insurance; and perform other vital activities to help individuals remain in their homes and communities for as long as possible (Accius, 2017; Redfoot, Feinberg, & Houser, 2013).

Although the "typical" family caregiver is a 49-year-old woman who takes care of a relative, men – a group traditionally not recognized for performing caregiving tasks – are rising to the challenge (Accius, 2017; National Alliance for Caregiving [NAC] & American Association of Retired Persons [AARP], 2015). Gender roles have been studied as an issue in caregiving since the early 1980s, but only recently have researchers expanded the focus of their studies to include men in caregiving roles (Arber, Gilbert, & Evandrou, 1988; Harris, 1998; Kaye & Applegate, 1990a, 1990b). In 2015, 40% of family caregivers were men, or there were 16 million male family caregivers in the United States. Approximately 56% of male caregivers are married, and the average age for a male family caregiver is 48 years old. About 23% of care recipients had Alzheimer's or experienced mental confusion (Accius, 2017). There is also great variation by age and the relationship between the caregiver and the care recipient. For example, 28% of all male family caregivers are millennials, and the average age for this group is 27 years old. The average age for a son caring for a parent or in-law is 46 years old, while that of a male family caregiver caring for a spouse/partner is 63 years old (National Alliance for Caregiving NAC and AARP Public Policy Institute, 2015).

Research statistics suggest that husbands and sons may assume different caregiving roles and may respond to the caregiving experiences in different ways (Chang & White-Means, 1991). Most studies of male caregivers have focused on the role of husband caregivers. Husbands make up 36% of spousal caregivers (Stone, Cafferata, & Sangl, 1987) and provide long hours of consistent and dependable care for their wives (Chang & White-Means, 1991; Johnson, 1983), often without assistance from others (Kaye & Applegate, 1990a; Stone et al., 1987). However, there are sons who are also actively involved in caregiving. Studies that make the distinction between primary and secondary caregivers have found that sons comprise 10%–12% of primary caregivers and 52% of secondary caregivers to elderly adults (Stone et al., 1987; Tennstedt, McKinlay, & Sullivan, 1989). Demographic and social trends, such as the growing elderly population, smaller average family sizes (resulting in fewer siblings available for elder care), greater sibling mobility, and changing gender roles contribute to the growing number of sons who will become caregivers to their elderly parents. Research on sons has been limited, and there is a gap in knowledge regarding sons in their caregiving roles. Studies found that the issues of bathing and driving were the most difficult caregiving tasks to handle for sons (Harris, 1998). Sons without any prior caregiving experience often find themselves taking over the enormous task of managing their parents' every need. Sons, like most other caregivers, also find themselves dealing with health care and social service systems that are confusing, expensive, and difficult to access (Harris, 1998).

African American Male Alzheimer's Caregivers

Scant research has been conducted on African American male caregivers (Crocker-Houde, 2001). Sixty-five percent of African Americans are more likely to be primary caregivers compared to Latinos (63%), Whites (53%), or Asian Americans (48%) (National Alliance for Caregiving NAC and AARP Public Policy Institute, 2015). Roughly 13% of male caregivers are African American. African American families care for their loved ones in the home at a much higher rate than other racial or ethnic groups. Long-term care outside of the home or community is typically the last resort. African American family dementia caregivers are more likely to keep their impaired elderly relatives at home longer, prior to nursing home admission, than Whites (Miller & Mukherhjee, 1999). They do so in spite of a heavier caregiving load in the area of activities of daily living care and emotional support (Navaie-Waliser, 2001; Wallsten, 2000).

Communities of color have a substantially higher risk of developing Alzheimer's and other dementias. African Americans are nearly two times more likely to develop Alzheimer's disease than White Americans. One of the greatest challenges in effectively addressing this disease is access to an early or timely dementia diagnosis. Communities of color continue to be underdiagnosed (WAI, n.d.). Stephenson (2001) reported that "African Americans stand a greater chance of being misdiagnosed and mistreated by the very people who are supposed to help them" (p. 779). The racial bias of health care providers experienced by these families may be attributed to a variety of factors that range from the screening tests used to detect early dementia to caregiver perception of covert racism or cultural insensitivity demonstrated by certain health care professionals. Misdiagnosis can be traumatic for the patient and family and further undermine the mistrust that many African Americans have in the health care system (Cloutterbuck & Mahoney, 2003; Stephenson, 2001, p. 779). Studies also indicate that primary care physicians dismissed caregivers' concerns about memory loss and/or behavioral changes in a loved one and instead focused on chronic conditions or misdiagnosed their family member (Hughes, Tyler, Danner, & Carter, 2009). Caregivers described interactions with health care providers that consistently denigrated, devalued, and disrespected their observations and concerns about their demented loved ones. They reported feeling diminished when physicians glibly dismissed or did not take their concerns seriously (Cloutterbuck & Mahoney, 2003). Further, a delay of almost seven years was found between symptom onset, problem recognition, and physician consultation. Lack of access to knowledgeable physicians in minority communities is another major barrier to the diagnostic process.

Studies have found that African Americans are diagnosed with Alzheimer's at later stages of the disease and present with greater impairment when compared to their White counterparts (Dilworth-Anderson, Williams, & Gibson, 2002; Shadlen, Larson, Gibbons, McCormick, & Teri, 1999). Overwhelmingly, informal networking is the most influential facilitator to obtaining a diagnosis for their loved one's cognitive and behavioral change. Diagnoses lead to clear, unambiguous communication with health and social service providers and referral to/coordination of support services, which greatly facilitate understanding of what is happening to their loved one's health. Typically, African American family caregivers are not knowledgeable about Alzheimer's disease prior to their family member having been diagnosed. Qualitative studies indicated that they were familiar with the word *Alzheimer's* but were not familiar with the symptoms, progression, or behavioral outcomes of the disease.

Because of the devastating effect on physical, mental, and social function in Alzheimer's disease, these caregivers often are subjected to significant caregiving burden (Alzheimer's Association, 2011). However, Alzheimer's caregiver burden and coping research has focused heavily on female caregivers, leaving the perspective from male caregivers an under-researched area (Geiger, Wilks, Lovelace, Chen, & Spivey, 2015). Male caregivers face caregiving burdens, have weak support networks, and are less likely to seek out programs that increase their caregiving capabilities and help them cope with this burden (Lopez–Anuarbe & Kohli, 2019). Over the progressive course of Alzheimer's disease, a continuum of services is needed to assist caregivers in coping with the changing demands of the patient. Yet studies continue to indicate that male caregivers, especially African American males, use few programs (Cox, 1999). Pinquart and Sorensen (2004) stated that higher levels of illness and disability among ethnic minorities would suggest higher levels of formal services used by minority caregivers: however, they underuse these services. This finding may stem from several factors: accessibility, language barriers, and limited financial resources. In addition, predisposing factors that contribute to less service use by minority caregivers may include cultural unacceptability of nursing home use (Pinquart & Sorensen, 2004).

Practice

The Wisconsin Alzheimer's Institute (WAI) is committed to helping people living with Alzheimer's disease or other dementia, their caregivers, and the health professionals working to support them. The mission is to promote health equity and improve the quality of life of people living with Alzheimer's disease and other dementias and their families through research and community engagement. The purpose is to increase dementia awareness; provide education on Alzheimer's disease and related disorders; identify and disseminate strategies to reduce dementia risk; convene stakeholders across the state; improve access to quality dementia care services; and develop and support culturally tailored, effective clinical and community-based models of care.

WAI Regional Milwaukee Office

In 2008, as part of a collaborative effort involving funding from Bader Philanthropies, the University of Wisconsin School of Medicine and Public Health (UWSMPH), the WAI, the WAI Regional Milwaukee office was created. The WAI Regional Milwaukee Office was established to address dementia in African American communities using an asset-based Community Development Model (ABCD) (Green-Harris et al., 2019) in alignment with the Wisconsin idea of ensuring all people in Wisconsin had access to fair equitable health service. It was also in alignment with each institutions' goal to improve the lives of older adults in southeastern Wisconsin impacted by Alzheimer's disease and other dementias. WAI's Regional Milwaukee office is centered on five integrated mission pillars: community outreach, professional education, advocacy, service, and research. This model empowers the Milwaukee and Southeastern Wisconsin communities of color, primarily African Americans, to actively participate by providing culturally specific health care services for their aging populations affected by dementia, Alzheimer's disease, and other health disparities (Wisconsin Alzheimer's Institute, n.d.). The WAI Regional Milwaukee Office works to reduce the stigma of and raise awareness about dementia, ensure access to early detection and diagnoses, and provide access to supportive services for those diagnosed and caregivers in African American and other underserved and underrepresented communities. The program works to reduce the health disparities faced by African Americans around Alzheimer's disease by developing and implementing culturally tailored approaches and techniques for those diagnosed, elders, and families at risk for Alzheimer's disease.

The WAI Regional Milwaukee office has worked with families in need of diagnosis and supportive services. The Milwaukee team is composed of five staff members, two of whom are solely committed to outreach and community engagement. We have staff identified as connectors whose focus is working with families in the trenches of dementia either as a person with a diagnosis, a caregiver, or both using a culturally tailored approach. Our model provides a comprehensive one-stop service for our families, is not income-based, and does not charge a fee for services. We start with in-home assessments to capture data and offer assistance with connecting families to our diagnostic memory clinics for care and diagnosis, followed by aftercare connection with ongoing supportive services until they are stable for at least 90 days or longer if needed. With this model, we have increased our presence and visibility both with providers and families. The WAI Milwaukee coordinator is often call on by providers and physicians to do home checks, or patient compliance checks. We have established relationships with social service, legal agencies, and other partners such as health care organizations, diagnostic memory clinics, the Aging Disability Resource Centers, and local ethnic coalitions and groups. These relationships have been instrumental to bridge partnerships to help community-based programs that connect with the African American community to reduce stigma, improve access to diagnoses, and improve overall health outcomes and provide better services to our families.

The WAI Regional Milwaukee office's initiative has resulted in the increase of African Americans becoming aware of Alzheimer's disease (AD), getting earlier detection and diagnosing, which has led to increased education and accessing supporting services for folks living with dementia and their families. In addition, this program has increased the level of understanding of the impact of AD in the African American community and reduced stigma about the disease. The WAI Regional Milwaukee office continues to build partnerships with and participate in multiple community events with agencies, continues to build new strategic partnerships in Milwaukee and Southeastern Wisconsin, and has been nationally recognized for its community engagement and program strategies. We provide awareness, education, outreach, and understanding of these significant health disparities facing communities of color. Our efforts focus on dementia-related early detection or risk reduction, treatment, psycho-social management, and caregiver interventions.

The Milwaukee Program's professional training consists of state-of-the-art education around best practices to provide culturally sensitive care to patients and effectively address community and family needs. Professional training is a critical component to the work: early on, the WAI Milwaukee office recognized the need for cultural inclusion training across health care systems and within community-based organizations. As the caregivers became savvier, and started asking more questions, they reported a noticeable difference in the attitudes of their providers. We were encouraging caregivers to ask questions about supportive services, clarification of diagnosis, how to cope as caregivers, etc., and caregivers were coming back to us sharing that their providers were uncomfortable answering their questions and often avoided the conversations. We further noticed that community-based organizations that were labeled as dementia-friendly were not well equipped to work with communities of color. They were offering very generic, non-ethnic service models that were not inclusive of beliefs, cultures, or values of non-majority populations. The day programs, for example, were not inclusive of cultural songs or stories. Staff were not familiar with cultural literature, activities, or important dates, and they were not used to interfacing with people from other cultures, which was troubling for African American caregivers because they noticed a difference in the care and treatment their loved ones were receiving. For example, staff that were interfacing with families were not trained in cultural communication styles and would use inappropriate titles or unknowingly use offensive terms when referring to something about the person. It was also noted that they would treat male caregivers differently, making assumptions that they could not provide adequate care for their loved one. As the complaints continued to increase over time, it was clear we needed to move upstream and assist our families by building the capacity of the workforce. We then developed and implemented three new training programs: The Faces of Aging in the 21st Century, Working with an Intergenerational Workforce, and How to Adapt New Practices of Inclusion. These trainings were cultural inclusion trainings that used very engaging practices and everyday examples of cultural biases that caregivers were reporting. We focused initially on frontline staff who had direct daily contact with African American families. As the program continued, in order to maximize the effectiveness of the model, we used a multi-team approach that included a patient-care model approach and included health teams. This approach could include social workers, providers, medical assistants, etc. This resulted in improved credibility and support from providers and attendees.

Examples of WAI Milwaukee Programs and Services

Milwaukee Health Services-Diagnostic Memory Clinic

Since 2009, the WAI Regional Milwaukee Office and Milwaukee Health Services (MHSI), Inc. have worked collectively to design a culturally tailored diagnostic memory clinic to serve African Americans in Milwaukee's vulnerable populations. This was the first African American-based memory clinic in the State of Wisconsin and the first Federally Qualified Health Center in Wisconsin that focused on African Americans. This clinic lead to increased diagnoses of African Americans, providers educated in AD, and resources for caregivers. In addition to working with the families in the community, the family care coordinator works directly with the WAI-affiliated Dementia Diagnostic Clinic at MHSI to provide in-home follow-up and outreach services to families. Through this program, MHSI has provided diagnostic and follow-up clinical services outreach services to more than 500 families. These services have included, but are not limited to, functional screenings for those reporting memory issues; coordination of medical care; connections with community programs and long-term care resources; and referrals to partner organizations such as the Milwaukee County Department on Aging, the Alzheimer's Association, Community Cares, and other aging organizations.

*Memory Diagnostic Clinic Community Program (the Dementia
Wellness Program)*

In 2014, with grant funding, the program expanded the reach of the Memory Assessment Clinic from inside of the clinic walls into the community. The program was able to develop the Dementia Wellness Program (DWP). DWP was designed to work with our most vulnerable elders to provide them with education, testing, and self-empowerment through lifestyle intervention classes in hopes of increasing awareness, reducing risks, and establishing a direct line to care and to achieve early detection for those who may have some form of cognitive impairment. The program consisted of a comprehensive screening ranging from blood pressure testing, glucose, stress levels, mini-mental state exams, and caregiver burden scales. This all leads to the participants enrolling in a six-week lifestyle intervention class for family caregivers and folks at higher risk of developing dementia. With continued funding we have been able to do the following:

- Provide memory screenings to more than 800 people living in underserved communities.
- Help connect elders without a health care home to primary care physicians.
- Increase public education and awareness about dementia and brain health.
- Identify folks who are at increased risk for dementia and provide them with supportive services to get an official diagnosis and full memory analysis.

Healthy Body/Healthy Mind Connection (HBHMC)

Train-the-trainer Dementia Wellness Program is for African American elders who are at risk for developing Alzheimer's disease. Building on the DWP, HBHMC is an innovative program that was designed based on BE WISE, an evidence-based curriculum developed through WISEWOMAN, the Centers for Disease Control and Prevention's (CDC's) national cardiovascular risk reduction program for women. HBHMC combines five weekly two-hour group education and skill-building sessions with health coaching and SMART goal follow-up. Intended outcomes include increased knowledge of dementia risk and preventive behaviors, self-efficacy to engage in preventive behaviors, improved dietary behavior and increased physical activity, and improved self-management of chronic conditions. With a tailored participant manual and tools to support behavior change, the program has been co-facilitated by staff of Milwaukee Health Services, Inc. and the WAI Milwaukee office and implemented in seven primarily African American senior housing sites and one senior center in Milwaukee's highest need areas.

PASSPORT Project–WAI Milwaukee and Milwaukee Health Services, Inc. Collaborative

As the WAI continues to provide services to individuals and families in the community, there is a growing need to connect seniors who may be at an increased risk for dementia with services. The PASSPORT Project is a community-based outreach education and supportive service intervention that serves to improve diagnosis and delay the onset of dementia in the African American community in Milwaukee. Through this unique program, we bring a physician, nurse practitioner, medical assistant, outreach worker, and student interns into the senior community living setting to provide talks, health screenings, group education, and lifestyle classes along with supportive services to our seniors in the comfort of their living space. The team (WAI and MHSI) performs a one-month and three-month follow-up with the participants to assess for behavior change; healthy lifestyle goal achievement; and changes in health including their blood pressure, cholesterol, blood sugar, and body mass index (BMI). This project was funded by the University of Wisconsin's School of Medicine and Public Health's Wisconsin Partnership Program.

The Amazing Grace Chorus® Program

Started in 2014 and modeled after Dr. Mary Mittleman's Unforgettables Caregiver Chorus model in New York, this program was funded by Bader Philanthropies. The Amazing Grace Chorus® is a culturally tailored program that aims to improve the quality of life of persons living with dementia and their caregivers through socialization and music. This program engages and provides support to African Americans and other underrepresented populations to increase public awareness of the importance of understanding how to help families living with dementia. This program is also structured to provide caregivers access to resources to support their loved ones and keep them in the home, as safe as possible for as long as possible. The coordinator is uniquely poised to assist the caregivers with a full spectrum of coordinated care services from newly diagnosed and learning to navigate services to end-of-life hospice care. Program goals include reducing the stigma associated with dementia, increasing dementia awareness, and identifying educational opportunities for participants to learn about health conditions and lifestyle factors that impact risk for memory loss. The program raises awareness on the higher prevalence of dementia amongst African Americans and demonstrates the commitment the University of Wisconsin (UW) and WAI have to address AD in African American communities.

Breaking the Silence Minority Health Month (MHM) Events

After working in the Milwaukee community for six years to the establish a foundation to reduce stigma, increase awareness, and help families on the dementia journey find appropriate paths to diagnosis, care, and support, we recognized that there needed to be something to highly visible to bring the community together to address the devastating impact that dementia is having in our communities of color. In 2014, the WAI Regional Milwaukee Office, with the support of Bader Philanthropies (formerly Helen Bader Foundation) and other partners, launched our first Minority Health Month (MHM) Breakfast Dialogue, Breaking the Silence: Addressing Dementia in Communities of Color.

The program was designed using the strength of the community partners to design the Breakfast Dialogue to ensure that it would have depth and impact in all communities of color. The goal of the dialogue is to help families suffering in silence have a voice and join in the discussion about its impact and to offer them hope and support as they go through this disease journey with their loved ones. By having community leaders and role models of color who have experienced dementia firsthand share their story, we hope to build awareness and reduce the stigma associated with the disease and help communities reach out for help for themselves and their loved ones living with the memory issues.

The MHM Dialogues have been extremely successful with about 500 attendees. Each year we increase our attendance, and our evaluations are favorable, with participants requesting that we continue our efforts the following year. Breaking the Silence is the first and only MHM event in the State of Wisconsin that focuses on dementia as a public health issue and more specifically the only one designed for communities of color.

WAI Regional Milwaukee Office Community Advisory Board

At the inception of the WAI Regional Milwaukee Office in 2008, the Community Advisory Board (CAB) was formed to be a voice to, and from, the community. This board meets monthly and serves as counsel to UW and WAI

Regional Milwaukee Office team on outreach, research, and retention/recruitment strategies and advises on barriers to research participation. The missions of our CAB are the following:

- Provide a voice for the community.
- Counsel the UW and WAI team on outreach and research recruitment strategies that are culturally sensitive.
- Identify and address barriers to research participation by underrepresented populations.
- Support the recruitment and retention of research subjects.
- Become a conduit for supporting community-based participatory research (CBPR) in the community.

The CAB is well regarded by scientist across multiple institutions and has been recognized as a key stakeholder for community engagement to bring culturally tailored programs into the African American community. This CAB was designed to be a support for people living with dementia and their caregivers to have a voice in programing, community engagement, and research. This group was designed to help caregivers have options in developing culturally tailored approaches that would be palatable and beneficial as they were on their caregiver journey. This CAB provides meaningful insight and support to investigators on research projects; resulting in funding for those projects provided by the National Institutes of Health (NIH) and has been recognized by the UW and Aurora researchers and NIH for its expertise and recommendations on innovative research proposals for the African American community. Additionally, their guidance was instrumental in the UW hiring an African American scientist in Alzheimer's disease and remains an integral part of the design and implementation process.

With a motto of "meet the people where they are" and the moral compass of the WAI Milwaukee CAB, WAI Milwaukee has been able to successfully align the work to mirror the needs of our community. For example, the dementia wellness program Healthy Body, Healthy Mind was developed from the BE WISE, CDC WISEWOMAN's cardiovascular program; while the model had been culturally adapted, as it was designed for African American women, it was critical to have male engagement. With the support from the community, the model was modified to be inclusive for men to participate, which had resulted in male participation. With the WAI's Amazing Grace Chorus Program®, the coordinator created a space for the men in the group to bond together and share among themselves using support mechanisms that promote bonding unique to their needs. We also have three male conductors leading the chorus, and this helps the male caregivers stay involved and engaged. At the inception of our program, we took on the model, "meet the people where they are." These are examples of how this program took intentional steps to and support the needs of our caregivers in a way that is beneficial to them and has resulted in long-term enrollment with our activities. Because this program listened to the community's voice and honored its request to develop and institute long-term programming based on their needs, this progam office is considered a pillar of support to the African American community by both families and providers. The WAI Milwaukee office is considered a valuable, dependable, and trustworthy resource for African American families to access for culturally appropriate support and services. This work has also resulted in improved health outcomes, reduction of stress in caregivers, mood enhancement of those living dementia, and the WAI Milwaukee becoming a staple and exemplary model for other organizations to follow.

Case Study

The client is a 44-year-old African American father of four. His mother lived on her own and had diabetes. She was saying weird things and was not managing her diabetes. She got ulcers on the bottom of her feet and it was recommended that they amputate one leg. Her family, which consisted of the client and his two sisters, asked if they could save the leg, so they put the leg in a cast to see if ulcers would subside but they would have to maintain her sugar levels. His mother had a medical background but would drink soda and smoke cigarettes. Initially, she did start to take care of herself, but they did not know that she was forgetting to take care of herself. Eventually, the doctors had to start removing her toes because of the diabetes. She went into recovery after surgery and had a smile on her face but did not say anything. The doctors said it was just the anesthesia, so they took her home. However, she did not call and when they went to check on her, she had the same clothes on, same smile, and her legs were bloody. They took her to the doctor, and the doctor came back after an hour and said she has dementia and can no longer take care of herself or live by herself. There was no explanation about what dementia meant and no education about the disease. Because of her age (55 years old), she was not eligible to go to a nursing home. The middle sister took her first to stay with her and other siblings helped. One challenge was that his mother would want to constantly eat and would say she was hungry all day, even if she had already eaten, and she had mood swings. This was shared with the doctor, who gave her a high dose of narcotic medication instead of resources. For five years, it was trial and error as they tried to take care of her.

Nevertheless, the siblings had a system for taking care of their mother. One sister had left the state, so the other sister with whom the mother lived had power of attorney. The client took care of his mother over the weekend by bringing his mother to his home and providing full care, including bathing, meal preparation, clothing, etc. He did all the care during his time, however, his sister received help with care. He realized he was the only one doing the bathing and did not complain because he knew his sister needed a break.

As a father, he did not feel comfortable asking his partner or children to help with care, so the caregiver burden and strain was heavy. When he got married, he introduced his wife to his mother. He stated that it seemed like his mother would only have an outburst when he was not around. However, he did not want his wife or children to say anything negative about his mother. Thus, his family had their world and he was alone caring for his mother. It was hard for him to know that his children did not see his mother as their "grandma." He could not talk to wife at the time and she did not give support.

He felt that taking care of his mother was his responsibility. He was used to seeing his mother as a matriarch who took care of everything. His father was not around, so having to provide care for someone who had taken care of everybody was challenging. There were times when he would become frustrated because his mother could not communicate and there were incontinence issues. Having to deal with the acidy smell of urine, bathing, and cleaning up the bed was frustrating. Afterwards, he would feel guilty for being angry or frustrated with his mother. However, there was no one he could talk to in his immediate circle, and if he tried to express his feelings to his siblings, it sounded like he was complaining. He internalized a lot.

There was a time where he had to step away from caregiving – he had a new son, was in a relationship, only had one car, and was driving 250 miles every day from his home to his sister's to make sure his mother was doing well. It was impacting his relationship, causing strains and issues, and again there was no one to talk to. Unfortunately, his mother became a double amputee because of the infections in her legs. Therefore, she was not able to come out of his sister's home as regularly. As a result, he decided to step away from the caregiving in his home. He felt guilty because he felt like he abandoned his sister and mother.

He found out about resources when he started working for Milwaukee County. He learned about services and then got upset because the doctor did not tell or connect them. It had been five to six years when he discovered these resources. However, when he brought the information to his sister about programs and services, he was met with resistance. She felt that they had a system in place and "knew what they were doing." She had developed a deeper bond with their mother and felt he was interrupting and causing tension by introducing new services. Since she had power of attorney, he could not make the decisions about care.

He was able to attend WAI Milwaukee's Annual Minority Health Month Breakfast. This connected him to resources to get a real diagnosis for his mother. Initially, they were not told what type of dementia she had. They focused on her memory but that was not what she needed. She had frontotemporal dementia, which affected her behaviors, executive functioning, and emotions. This would have been helpful to know and would have prevented anger and frustration, especially when his mother could not express herself when she had to use the bathroom.

Strategies

This case study holds several implications for those working with African American male caregivers and their families. It is critical to develop gender and culturally sensitive interventions and modes of caregiver support. By being aware of possible racial, ethnic, and cultural variations in the caregiving experience, health care providers can better meet the needs of the diverse groups of caregivers they serve (Cox & Monk, 1996). Communities of color may resist services or experience barriers to access. Therefore, when African American family caregivers typically engage in services, it is in crisis or when caregivers have reached burnout. Although difficulties in leaving their relative may not prohibit use, feelings of being overwhelmed may affect any inclination to attempt a new service. Follow-up contacts, including home visits that encourage utilization and offer support, may help encourage service use. It is imperative to recognize that caregivers with the greatest needs may also have the greatest difficulties in following through on their intended plans. Likewise, it is important to recognize that similar factors may be inhibiting use by diverse groups of caregivers, and thus procedures that immediately link caregivers with services are needed (Cox, 1999). This case study demonstrated that the family caregivers needed more education and information *earlier*.

Zarit and Femia (2008) identified several aspects associated with effective interventions for caregivers. These characteristics include a combined psychological and educational approach and a multidimensional perspective. The intervention should be tailored to address the caregiver's specific needs and stressors and should be flexible to fit the caregiver throughout the treatment (Zarit & Femia, 2008; Farcnik & Persyko, 2002; Geiger et al., 2015). More educational support groups, respite programs, and other support groups for male caregivers, especially African American sons caring for a parent with Alzheimer's are needed (Mathew, Mattocks, & Slatt, 1990; Barton & Williams, 2003; Weinland, 2009). Clinicians might assess male caregivers' burden and help identify maladaptive coping strategies. To assess the African American male caregiver, providers have to build trust to make the caregiver feel comfortable with sharing the "real situation." African American male caregivers should also be given the opportunity to give back through sharing their experiences without being judged.

Comprehensive assessments of caregivers and care recipients and the identification of perceived needs will provide important information. Resources and support should be tailored to the caregiver–recipient relationship. Individuals caring for spouses have a different situation than a child caring for a parent. Sons, in general, do not have strong friendship networks (Harris, 1998). Many confide in their wives or significant others, but they do not have any other outlets for the multitude of feelings with which they are dealing. Providers need to expand their understanding of the roles of sons as caregivers. They must listen to sons' concerns, identify

sons' strengths, and recognize sons' diversity. Going against gender stereotypes, some sons are deeply involved in caring for a parent with AD. As
the baby boomers come of age, more sons will find themselves in caregiving roles, and services to aid, support, and encourage this care need to
be in place.

Lessons Learned

When working with African American families, typically caregiving of
loved ones with AD is provided as a unit. There are multiple caregivers in
the family and each person has his or her own experience in providing that
care. Providers must not assume that sons are not involved in the care of
their parents, and they must assess that individuals' caregiving burden and
needs. Regarding environmental changes needed, a unique challenge for
male caregivers was being able to take a parent or loved one of another sex
to the restroom. Restaurants rarely have bathrooms where a male caregiver
could go into the restroom to assist his mother. Therefore, this requires an
environmental change in these settings or other family settings to ensure
that family or private unisex restrooms are available.

Preventing and addressing family and systems conflict remains an overlooked yet potentially critical component of clinical care in dementia.
Academic and clinical attention has been directed mostly to caregiver stress
or burden, and usually the focus has been on the effect of family conflict on
the primary caregiver rather than on the family system as a whole and the
intra-familial dynamics (Brodaty & Hadzi-Pavlovic, 1990; Brodaty &
Green, 2002; Pinquart & Sorensen, 2004; Schulz & Martire, 2004; Depp,
Sorocco, & Kasl-Godley, 2005; Mittelman, Ferris, & Shulman, 1996;
Mitrani, Feaster, & McCabe, 2005). However, studies show that family
conflict was most commonly seen in families caring for loved ones with
mild to moderate dementia and most frequently the conflict is between
siblings. Common themes included accusations of neglect, exploitation,
lack of communication, or sequestration of the person with dementia
(Peisah, Brodaty, & Quadrio, 2006). Harris (1998) found that having
parents with dementia affected caregiving sons' sibling relationships. A
parent's illness brought some siblings closer together. They talked more
over the phone and saw each other frequently, sometimes daily. In other
cases, the tensions brought on by the parent's illness reawakened old sibling
rivalries, often accompanied by a sibling's refusal to accept responsibility in
the parent's care, pushing the siblings even further apart. Sons often expressed difficulty in accepting the fact that they now had to take on many
of the roles and tasks that their parents had performed for them as children.
It is critical for providers to ask about and discuss family conflict with
African American male caregivers to ensure that the appropriate supports
are recommended.

54 *Latrice Rollins and Gina Green-Harris*

References

Accius, J. (2017). Breaking stereotypes: Spotlight on male family caregivers. *AARP Public Policy Institute*, 26, 1–6.

Arber, S., Gilbert, G.N., & Evandrou, M. (1988). Gender, household composition and receipt of domiciliary services by elderly disabled people. *Journal of Social Policy*, 17, 153–175.

Alzheimer's Association. (2011). Alzheimer's disease facts and figures. Retrieved from http://www.alz.org/downloads/Facts_Figures_2011.pdf .

Ballard, E.L., Nash, F., Raiford, K., & Harrell, L.E. (1993). Recruitment of black elderly for clinical research studies of dementia: The CERAD experience. *The Gerontologist*, 33, 561–565.

Barton, P., & Williams, E. (2003). Successful support groups for African American caregivers. *Generations*, 27(4), 81–83.

Brodaty, H., & Green, A. (2002). Defining the role of the caregiver in Alzheimer's disease treatment. *Drugs Aging*, 19, 891–898.

Brodaty, H., & Hadzi-Pavlovic, D. (1990). Psychosocial effects on carers of living with persons with dementia. *Australian and New Zealand Journal of Psychiatry*, 24, 351–361.

Chang, C.F., & White-Means, S.I. (1991). The men who care: An analysis of male primary caregivers who care for frail elderly at home. *The Journal of Applied Gerontology*, 10, 343–358.

Cloutterbuck, J., & Mahoney, D.F. (2003). African American dementia caregivers: The duality of respect. *Dementia*, 2(2), 221–243.

Cox, C. (1999a). Race and caregiving: patterns of service use by African American and White caregivers of persons with Alzheimer's disease. *Journal of Gerontological Social Work*, 32(2), 5–19.

Cox, C. (1999b). Service needs and use: A further look at the experiences of African American and white caregivers seeking Alzheimer's assistance. *American Journal of Alzheimer's Disease*, 14(2), 93–101.

Cox, C., & Monk, A. (1996). Strain among caregivers: Comparing the experiences of African American and Hispanic caregivers of Alzheimer's relatives. *The International Journal of Aging and Human Development*, 43(2), 93–105.

Depp, C., Sorocco, K., Kasl-Godley, J., Thompson,L., Rabinowitz, Y., Gallagher-Thompson, D. (2005). Caregiver self-efficacy, ethnicity, and kinship differences in dementia caregivers. *American Journal of Geriatric Psychiatry*, 13, 787–794.

Crocker-Houde, S. (2001). Men providing care to older adults in the home. *Journal of Gerontological nursing*, 27(8), 13–19.

Dilworth-Anderson, P., Williams, I.C., & Gibson, B. (2002). Issues of race, ethnicity, and culture in caregiving research. *The Gerontologist*, 42, 237–272.

Farcnik, K., & Persyko, M.S. (2002). Assessment, measures and approaches to easing caregiver burden in Alzheimer's disease. *Drugs Aging*, 19(3), 203–215.

Geiger, J.R., Wilks, S.E., Lovelace, L.L., Chen, Z., & Spivey, C.A. (2015). Burden among male Alzheimer's caregivers: Effects of distinct coping strategies. *American Journal of Alzheimer's Disease & Other Dementias®*, 30(3), 238–246.

Green-Harris, G., Coley, S.L., Houston, S., Norris, N., & Edwards, D. (2018, July). Milwaukee melodies and memories chorus project: the amazing grace chorus: Developing a culturally- tailored lifestyle intervention program for African Americans with dementia and caregivers using an asset-based community development approach. In *33rd International Conference of ADI*. ADI.

Green-Harris, G., Coley, S.L., Koscik, R.L., Norris, N.C., Houston, S.L., Sager, M.A., & Edwards, D.F. (2019). Addressing disparities in Alzheimer's disease and African American participation in research: An asset-based community development approach. *Frontiers in Aging Neuroscience*, 11, 125.

Green-Harris, G., Corbett, M., Stehman, C., Houston, S., Skora, T., Wright, C., & Edwards, D. (2018, July). Connecting the dots part 2-the dementia wellness project: A culturally appropriate lifestyle intervention for African American elders at risk for dementia. In *33rd International Conference of ADI*. ADI.

Green-Harris, G., Koscik, R.L., Houston, S., Norris, N., Mahoney, J., Sager, M.A., & Edwards, D. F. (2017). Using asset-based community involvement to address health disparities and increase African American participation in AD research: Experiences from The Wisconsin Alzheimer's institute. *Alzheimer's & Dementia: The Journal of the Alzheimer's Association*, 13(7), P897–P898.

Harris, P.B. (1998). Listening to caregiving sons: Misunderstood realities. *The Gerontologist*, 38(3), 342–352.

Houde, S.C. (2002). Methodological issues in male caregiver research: An integrative review of the literature. *Journal of Advanced Nursing*, 40(6), 626–640. doi: 10.1046/j. 1365-2648.2002.02423.x.

Hughes, T., Tyler, K., Danner, D., & Carter, A. (2009). African American caregivers: An exploration of pathways and barriers to a diagnosis of Alzheimer's disease for a family member with dementia. *Dementia*, 8(1), 95–116.

Jackson, J.D., Buchwald, D., Cahan, V., Carrillo, M.C., Gladman, J.T., Green-Harris, G., … & Baker, L. (2018). *The national strategy for Alzheimer's disease clinical research recruitment & participation*. Retrieved from https://www.nia.nih.gov/sites/default/files/2018-10/ alzheimers-disease-recruitment-strategy-final.pdf.

Johnson, C.L. (1983). Dyadic family relations and social support. *The Gerontologist*, 23, 377–383.

Kaye, L.W., & Applegate, J.S. (1990a). *Men as caregivers to the elderly: Understanding and aiding unrecognized family support*. Lexington, MA: Lexington Books.

Lopez–Anuarbe, M., & Kohli, P. (2019). Understanding male caregivers' emotional, financial, and physical burden in the United States. *Healthcare*, 7(2), 72.

Mathew, L.J., Mattocks, K., & Slatt, L.M. (1990). Exploring the roles of men: Caring for demented relatives. *Journal of Gerontological Nursing*, 16(10), 20–25.

McDonnell, E., & Ryan, A.A. (2014). The experience of sons caring for a parent with dementia. *Dementia*, 13(6), 788–802.

Miller, B., & Mukherhjee, S. (1999). Service use, caregiving mastery, and attitudes toward community service. *Journal of Applied Gerontology*, 18, 162–176.

Mitrani, V.B., Feaster, D.J., McCabe, B.E., et al. (2005). Adapting the structural family systems rating to assess the patterns of interaction in families of dementia caregivers. *Gerontologist*, 45, 445–455.

Mittelman, M.S., Ferris, S.H., Shulman, E., et al. (1996). A family intervention to delay nursing home placement of patients with Alzheimer's disease: a randomised controlled trial. *Journal of the American Medical Association*, 276, 1725–1731.

National Alliance for Caregiving (NAC) and AARP Public Policy Institute, *Caregiving in the U.S. 2015* (Bethesda, MD: NAC, and Washington, DC: AARP, June 2015), Retrieved from http://www.aarp.org/content/dam/aarp/ppi/2015/caregiving-in-the-united-states-2015-report-revised.pdf.

Navaie-Waliser, M., Feldman, P.H., Gould, D.A., Levine, C., Kuerbis, A.N., & Donelan, K. (2001). The experiences and challenges of informal caregivers: common themes and differences among whites, blacks, and Hispanics. *The Gerontologist*, B41(6), 733–741.

Peisah, C., Brodaty, H., & Quadrio, C. (2006). Family conflict in dementia: prodigal sons and black sheep. *International Journal of Geriatric Psychiatry: A Journal of the Psychiatry of Late Life and Allied Sciences*, 21(5), 485–492.

Pinquart, M., & Sorensen, S. (2004). Associations of caregiver stressors and uplifts with subjective well-being and depressive mood: a meta-analytic comparison. *Aging Ment Health*, 8, 438–449.

Redfoot, D., Feinberg, L., & Houser, A. (2013). *The aging of the baby boom and the growing care gap: A look at future declines in the availability of family caregivers.* Washington, DC: AARP Public Policy Institute. Retrieved from http://www.aarp.org/content/dam/aarp/research/public_policy_institute/ltc/2013/baby-boom-and-the-growing-care-gap-insight-AARP-ppi-ltc.pdf.

Robinson, C.A., Bottorff, J.L., Pesut, B., Oliffe, J.L., & Tomlinson, J. (2014). The male face of caregiving: A scoping review of men caring for a person with dementia. *American Journal of Men's Health*, 8(5), 409–426.

Schulz, R., & Martire, L.M. (2004). Family caregiving of persons with dementia: Prevalence, health effects, and support strategies. *American Journal of Geriatric Psychiatry*, 12, 240–249.

Shadlen, M.F., Larson, E.B., Gibbons, L., McCormick, W.C., & Teri, L. (1999). Alzheimer's disease symptom severity in Blacks and Whites. *Journal of the American Geriatrics Society*, 47(4), 482–486.

Stephenson, J. (2001). Racial barriers may hamper diagnosis, care of patients with Alzheimer disease. *Journal of the American Medical Association*, 286(7), 779–780.

Stone, R., Cafferata, G., & Sangl, J. (1987). Caregivers of the frail elderly: A national profile. *The Gerontologist*, 29, 677–683.

Tennstedt, S.L., McKinlay, J.B., & Sullivan, L.M. (1989). Informal care for frail elders: The role of secondary caregivers. *The Gerontologist*, 29, 677–683.

Wallsten, S. S. (2000). Effects of caregiving, gender, and race on the health, mutuality, and social supports of older couples. *Journal of Aging & Health*, 12(1), 90–111.

Weinland, J.A. (2009). The lived experience of informal African American male caregivers. *American Journal of Men's Health*, 3(1), 16–24.

Wisconsin Alzheimer's Institute. (n.d.). Retrieved from https://wai.wisc.edu/milwaukee/.

Zarit, S., & Femia, E. (2008). Behavioral and psychosocial interventions for family caregivers. *American Journal of Nursing*, 108(9 suppl), 47–53.

5 Engaging and Working with African American Fathers in Prison

Fathers and Children Together Experience Initiative

Diane Aisha Sears

Introduction

During the last quarter of the 20th century and continuing into the millennium, fatherhood has become more than just about raising children. It has morphed into a movement – a global movement – driven by fathers, out of their need to create solutions and support services to help address the key challenges that make it difficult, if not impossible, to positively shape the minds and souls of their children. Incarcerated African American fathers are confronted with unique key challenges created by their set of circumstances. Some of these key challenges are articulated in an article entitled "A Spiritual Force," penned by Mr. David Lee, published in IN SEARCH OF FATHERHOOD®, a quarterly international fatherhood and men's issues journal:

> After thirteen staggering years after being hostilely extracted from my community and my beautiful daughter's life, I am still striving mentally to adjust to the psychologically scarring reality of me not having a presence in this precocious young life I have watched through the gateway of a moist, dark maternal gateway into this chaotic world. There have been countless nights of tossing and turning in some uncomfortable state-owned bed pondering or guessing what steps she might be taking while I waste away inside the swiftly growing "Prison Industrial Complex." Is her cultural, historical, technological, spiritual character and basic development being undertaken in a nurturing environment? Are there problems at school, or the local neighborhood occurring that would require the attention of a caring father?... I have sent home books and a weighty sum of mail with the hopes of conveying an undying love, nevertheless our relationship is still an uncertain odyssey in which we struggle to learn more about each other and the socioeconomic dynamics surrounding our unceremonious separation.
>
> (Lee, 2001, pp. 37–38)

When we look at fatherhood through the lens of incarcerated African American fathers, courtesy of Mr. Lee, we find that the shaping of their child's cultural, historical, technological, and spiritual character and basic development is a critical concern that weighs heavily on their minds. This critical concern becomes a key challenge for incarcerated African American fathers as they are not physically present in the life of their child to provide him or her with the type of psychological reinforcement and historical, spiritual, and cultural grounding the child will need to successfully navigate subliminal systemic racism. The geographical boundaries that separate the incarcerated African American father and his child serves as an obstacle to developing a strong bond between the two of them. Because of systemic racism, which is evidenced by, among other things, the steady diet of negative stereotypical portrayals of African American men and particularly incarcerated African American men that emanates from mainstream media, television, and film, developing a strong father-child bond is more of a critical path item for an incarcerated African American father than his in-carcerated counterparts who are members of other ethnic groups. Incarcerated African American fathers are plagued by the thought that their children may subliminally think less of them not only because they are absent from their lives but also because of the purposefully consistent ne-gative portrayals of African American males their child sees in newspaper headlines and television news broadcasts and hears on radio news broad-casts. They wonder: "Will my child think I am a monster? How can I get my child to see me for who I am – a man – not a monster – a father who loves them and desperately wants to maintain a parental bond?" For in-carcerated African American fathers, subliminal systemic racism even seeps into parenting. In addition to addressing the challenge of bonding with their child and maintaining a consistent presence in their child's life despite the geographical distance that exists between them, incarcerated African American fathers grapple with the unique challenge of preparing their child to navigate a society immersed in subliminal systemic racism and preventing them from becoming entangled in the "school-to-prison" pipeline. No other ethnic group of incarcerated fathers is saddled with this key challenge. Contrary to what you may believe, hear, read, or think about incarcerated African American fathers, these gentlemen love their children. They have the same dreams that other fathers have for their children – and even the same fears.

In 2012, a brilliant group of thought leaders at SCI Phoenix (formerly SCI Graterford), the largest male maximum security prison in the Commonwealth of Pennsylvania, designed and co-implemented a dynamic two-tiered par-enting initiative – Fathers And Children Together Experience (formerly, the FACT Initiative) –under the banner of the United Community Action Network (U-CAN). Members of U-CAN collaborated with the Latin American Cultural Exchange Organization (LACEO), an organization also located at SCI Phoenix, in co-implementing the FACT Experience Initiative.

U-CAN embarked on a mission to educate incarcerated men, through a series of powerful workshops, to become responsible fathers and help them establish or, in some cases, re-establish, a positive relationship with their child. Members of U-CAN saw a direct connection between fatherlessness, intergenerational incarceration, and the school-to-prison pipeline. The FACT Experience Initiative is a solution for ending fatherlessness, effectively addressing intergenerational incarceration, and enhancing public safety.

In November 2013, U-CAN extended an invitation to IN SEARCH OF FATHERHOOD®, which publishes the literary works of incarcerated fathers throughout the United States and for which I serve as ative managing editor, to enter into a collaboration. Without hesitation, I said: "Yes!" The collaborative role with U-CAN involved publishing infrmation about the FACT Experience Initiative in a quarterly international Fatherhood and Mens Issues journal and blog, *IN SEARCH OF FATHERHOOD(R)*.

Practice

The FACT Experience Initiative is a 13-week program that culminates with a graduation ceremony that presents certificates to fathers acknowledging their completion of the program. During the first six weeks of the program, incarcerated fathers receive intensive parenting training that includes co-parenting tools. The next seven weeks of the program bring together incarcerated fathers and their child on a weekly basis. One evening each week for six of the seven weeks, incarcerated fathers and their child bond with one another, talk to each other, and participate in workshops together. The fathers and children learn basic things about each other – their favorite colors, the foods they like to eat, and their favorite movies. Fathers and children participate in art classes and work together on arts and crafts projects provided by the Philadelphia Mural Arts Program (www.muralarts.org), which collaborates with the FACT Experience Initiative and U-CAN. The seventh and final week of the program is reserved for the fathers' graduation ceremony. Fathers who have completed the program receive a certificate in a ceremony that is attended by their children, their children's mother or legal guardian, family members, the prison's superintendent, and community stakeholders. On at least one occasion, the mayor of Pottstown, Pennsylvania attended the ceremony. On other occasions, the Pennsylvania Department of Corrections Secretary, the Honorable John E. Wetzel; and Mrs. Lorraine Ballard Morrill, News and Community Affairs Director at Power 99/ WUSL-FM, a popular Philadelphia radio station owned by Clear Channel Media and Entertainment, have appeared at a graduation ceremony.

Incarcerated fathers participating in the FACT Experience Initiative are carefully selected and vetted by members of U-CAN. An external group of key stakeholders is provided with the names of the incarcerated fathers, the identity and contact information for the mother or legal guardian of their child, and the child's name and age. The key stakeholders assist members of U-CAN with a series of critical tasks that include, among other things, the following:

- Contacting the mother or legal guardian (e.g., grandmother or aunt) of the incarcerated father's child for the purposes of having her participate in the program along with the child.
- Obtaining the child's mother or legal guardian's written permission that allows the child to participate in the program.
- Ensuring that the principal and/or duly designated administrative officer of the child's school has received legal documentation executed by the child's mother or legal guardian that certifies that permission is granted for the child to participate in the FACT Experience Initiative for seven weeks and to leave school early on a designated day during the seven-week period.
- Scheduling and coordinating activities for the orientation session for the FACT Experience Initiative that must be attended by the child and his or her mother or legal guardian.
- Initiating follow-up communications with members of U-CAN that provide a status report on the orientation session, which among other things, (a) confirms the names of the children and their mother or legal guardian who have agreed in writing to participate in the program, (b) advises whether or not the children and their mother or legal guardian attended the orientation session, and (c) verifies whether or not all of the appropriate paperwork for each child and their mother or legal guardian has been fully executed and submitted.
- Initiating calls with a child's mother or legal guardian days in advance of the child's scheduled visitation with his or her father to remind the child's mother or legal guardian of (a) the date and time that both she and the child have to be present at the designated location to board the van that will transport them to SCI Phoenix to participate in the program, (b) the prison's dress code, and (c) ensuring that the child is present at the designated location for the purposes of boarding the van that will transport him or her to the prison in the event the mother or legal guardian of the child is unable to participate in the program on a particular date.
- Initiating follow-up communications with members of U-CAN on a weekly basis to confirm that each individual child will be present at each forthcoming workshop and visitation with his or her father. Immediately after receiving a follow-up communication from the group of key stakeholders, members of U-CAN contact each father to advise him whether his child will be present at the forthcoming week's workshop at the prison.

The six-week program is divided into five sessions that occur twice a week for two hours from 1:00 P.M. through 3:00 P.M.:

Session One: An exploration of how fatherless households impact families and how and why it is a causative factor for the plethora of problems plaguing the African American community is undertaken.

Session Two: Fathers learned how to become accountable and responsible parents. The men learned that they could demonstrate accountability and responsibility to their children by, as an example, checking their homework. They learned that accountability and responsibility is about deeds and not words.

Session Three: The importance of education and talking to their child about education was explored with fathers. The fathers were also told that upon their release from prison that it was important to meet their child's principal and play a proactive role in their child's education by, among other things, reviewing their child's homework.

Session Four: This segment of the six-week parenting program, entitled "Bonding," pointed out to fathers that they were not taught how to bond with their child because many of them did not have fathers in their lives. The fathers learned that bonding with their child helped them as parents to find and know their child's strengths and weaknesses, likes and dislikes, and how to build a better relationship with them.

Session Five: This segment of the six-week parenting program, entitled "Love/Self Worth," constituted the final parenting workshop for the fathers. Fathers came away from this session with the clear understanding that they will need to help their child develop his or her self-worth and that it was their – the fathers'–responsibility to ensure that their child understands that he or she is worth much more than what they see every day in their community. Love was defined for the fathers as a verb – an "action" word. The fathers were told that parenting involves utilizing their listening skills; teaching their child how to love through their actions; and showing their child that they loved them by, among other things, supporting and listening to them.

While fathers at SCI Phoenix are undergoing intensive parenting training, miles away – in Philadelphia, Pennsylvania – the planning of the orientation session for children of these fathers and each child's mother or legal guardian begins. To accommodate the schedules of the children and their mother or legal guardian, the orientation sessions are always held on a Saturday, beginning at 10:00 A.M. and ending at 2:00 P.M. The orientation session provides a free breakfast and lunch; arts and crafts projects for the children courtesy of the Philadelphia Mural Arts Program; an overview of the FACT Experience Initiative; and a group counseling session that explores a myriad of issues that include, but are not limited to, co-parenting, the children's behavior and academic performance, and disciplining children. During the session, a discussion of the dress code for the children ensues. Mothers and legal guardians are reminded about the street address of the location of the vans and the time at which the vans will depart from the location to transport the children and their mothers and legal guardians to the prison. An alumni group consisting of mothers and legal guardians who are graduates of the FACT Experience Initiative are on hand. They talk to the new group of mothers and legal guardians who have enrolled in the program about how the program has positively changed their lives, their relationship with their child, their child's life, and their child's relationship with his or her father. Members of the alumni group provide their contact information to the new group of mothers and legal guardians and encourage them to call if they have questions or if they just need someone to talk to. It becomes clear to the new group of mothers and legal guardians that they now have a support system – something many of them never had.

I observed an orientation session – a series of small workshops – provided for mothers and legal guardians of children whose fathers were participating in the FACT Experience Initiative at SCI Phoenix. Mothers and legal guardians accompanied by their children streamed into a large meeting room on the first floor of a large building in the Cobbs Creek section of Philadelphia, Pennsylvania. Each mother and legal guardian was given an informational package containing literature about the FACT Experience Initiative and consent forms that were to be reviewed, completed, and submitted to a designated stakeholder for processing. The group of women who enrolled in the FACT Experience Initiative were mothers, grand-mothers, and aunts of the children who accompanied them – children who, by the end of the coming week, would be reunited with their fathers at SCI Phoenix. A light breakfast of danish, donuts, bagels, coffee, hot tea, and hot chocolate was served. I used the limited time to talk to as many of the mothers, grandmothers, and aunts that I could. I wanted to hear their stories. And the stories of these women were so similar. Some had enrolled their daughter or son, grandson or granddaughter, or niece or nephew in the program because the children were having academic or behavioral is-sues. Others told me that they wanted the child they had enrolled in the program to get to know his or her father. The children, on average, ranged in age from 7 through 15. They seemed to take in stride the fact that they would see their father in less than one week. I was struck by how non-chalant they seemed about an experience that would positively transform their lives.

At the conclusion of breakfast, the children are separated from their mothers and legal guardians. They are relocated to the rear of the large meeting room and participate in arts and craft projects administered by personnel from Mural Arts Philadelphia (https://www.muralarts.org). While the children created artwork, their mothers and legal guardians lis-tened to speakers who conducted a series of brief workshops. Parenting, building relationships, and stress were a few of the topics explored. The mothers and legal guardians were reminded that children see and hear everything, mimic their behavior and speech, and that they – the mothers and legal guardians – are their children's role models. They were cautioned to be aware of every aspect of their behavior and the manner in which they speak to their children. The importance of ensuring that children had contact with their incarcerated father was emphasized. Estranged relationships between mothers and fathers were not to be used as an excuse to deny children access to their incarcerated father. In addition to counseling sessions, the mothers and legal guardians learned that, if needed, they would also receive assistance in obtaining resources and support services. The mothers and legal guardians learned about one of the successes of the FACT Experience Initiative, which involved a behavioral change. A story was shared with the mothers and legal guardian about an incarcerated father who, before he enrolled in the FACT Experience Initiative, would spend the majority of his time on the telephone speaking with the mother of his child. After speaking with the mother of his child, he would engage his child in a discussion with the time he had remaining for the call. However, after participating in the intensive parenting program offered by the FACT Experience Initiative, the incarcerated father changed his behavior. He continued to place calls to the mother of his child, *but* he asked to speak with his child *first*. During every call, he immediately engaged his child in a discussion and after speaking with his child, he would then speak with the child's mother!

From time to time, the issues discussed during the workshops tugged at the women's heartstrings. Several were moved to tears. In just a short period of time, one could see a transformation in the women and in the children. The women who had walked into the orientation session somberfaced and reclusive were now smiling and talking to one another. And what about the children? The children who were nonchalant were now animated and exuberant and could be seen talking to and playing with each other. At the end of the arts and craft session, they enthusiastically greeted their mother or legal guardian and, with pride, displayed the artwork that they created. Smiles illuminated the faces of the children as they put on their coats, gathered their artwork, and talked excitedly with their mother or legal guardian. In just four hours, the FACT Experience Initiative – through an orientation session – had already positively transformed the mothers and legal guardians of the children and the children.

I witnessed the powerful impact of the FACT Experience Initiative. On a Friday afternoon in March 2014, an imam, a member of Philadelphia's interfaith community, along with me and a group of mothers, legal guardians, and children boarded a van in the Cobbs Creek section of Philadelphia, Pennsylvania. We were whisked to SCI Phoenix where children and their fathers were reunited under the auspices of the FACT Experience Initiative crafted by U-CAN. Mothers, legal guardians, and their children walked into the cavernous reception area of the high-ceilinged prison lobby. Corrections officers stationed at an elongated desk greeted us as they checked off the name of each child on the visitors list under the watchful eye of each mother and legal guardian. The children were issued wristbands that bore their typewritten names and their destination as the group of legal guardians and mothers returned to the van. They were being driven to a nearby restaurant for dinner and counseling session – the same counseling session that the children's fathers received. The dinner was paid for by the incarcerated fathers from their wages.

Corrections officers opened a huge metal door and escorted us into a room where we were greeted by another group of armed and solemn-faced corrections officers. Once we were all assembled in the room, the huge metal door shut behind us with an ear shattering force that rattled every fiber of my being. We removed our shoes and walked through a metal detector. After walking through the metal detector without incident, we reclaimed our shoes and were summoned to a far corner of the room where corrections officers performed "body scans" with a handheld metal detector. Having successfully undergone "body scans," we were fingerprinted. I was amazed at the mature level of calm and stoicism each child exhibited. They never recoiled – at least not physically – at the treatment they were receiving. I thought to myself: "Good grief! This is what every child has to go through if he or she wants to see an incarcerated parent?!" The room we currently occupied was the last gauntlet separating the children from their fathers.

As the huge metal door closed behind us with its customary earth-shattering force, the children, accompanied by the imam and me, silently made their way down a winding ramp leading to the prison's meeting room. The double doors to the meeting room were open. To the right of the meeting room's double doors was a large window. The incarcerated fathers were waiting patiently, crowded together, at the large window in the meeting room. When the men caught glimpses of the children walking toward the meeting room, a bright smile illuminated their faces. You could sense their joy. The room erupted into applause. Yes, the men gave the children a standing ovation as they walked through the doors and into the room! And the children smiled broadly, waved to them, and ran into their outstretched arms. After greeting each other with hugs and kisses, the fathers and children sat down together at tables where they ate snacks and talked.

An interactive workshop was conducted with the fathers and the children by three co-facilitators, under the watchful eye of members of U-CAN. The fathers and children were asked to sit in chairs arranged in a large circle. To relieve the stress and tension that developed as the fathers waited patiently, but anxiously, for the children's arrival, coupled with the long ride to SCI Phoenix the children had endured, a relaxation technique was implemented. Everyone was instructed to hold the hand of the person sitting next to them, to take a deep breath and inhale and to, after a few seconds, exhale. The facilitator of the interactive workshop explained to the fathers and children that the inhalation and exhalation of oxygen has a calming effect. They were encouraged to utilize this technique when they felt anxious or stressful. Next, the children and their fathers were instructed to stand up and stretch their arms upward and then move them in a circular motion. Here again, fathers and children were receiving a valuable lesson on how to relieve anxiety and stress.

Co-facilitators of the workshop asked the children to express their feelings. They were given permission to talk about the emotions they were feeling on the long trip to SCI Phoenix. One child stated that she thought about writing a letter to her father because the trip seemed so long. She also stated that she was frustrated at having to wait so long to see her father. This revelation moved the co-facilitators to ask each father and each child to describe the emotions they felt while they waited to see each other. The children stated that they felt frustrated, anxious, and stressful while traveling to SCI Phoenix. Fathers discussed their emotions. They felt frustrated, anxious, and stressful and were worried about their children. One of the workshop co-facilitators pointed out to the group that an interesting lesson could be learned. And that lesson was that both fathers and children experience the same range of emotions. The exercise also pointed out that there is a need to provide children with an opportunity to articulate their emotions. At the same time, this exercise also taught children how to constructively express their feelings.

Each father and child was asked to stand up and introduce each other to the group. One by one, each father introduced himself by providing his name. He then turned to his son or daughter and introduced him or her to the group. Each child introduced himself or herself to the group, and then turned to gaze into the face of his or her father while proudly declaring to the group, "This is my father!"

The final exercise involved each father standing up, facing his child, and speaking from his heart to his child. There were three dramatically moving moments that occurred during this intense exercise:

A father stood up, faced his teenaged daughter, and told her: "I was not there when you were born. I was not there when you took your first step or on your first day of school. I will not be there to see you graduate. But I love you."

The sole grandfather in the group stood up and talked to his granddaughter, who was too emotionally overcome to stand in front of the group. As she sat in her chair weeping silently, he talked about the fact that he had been incarcerated for 23 years, that he hoped to leave prison soon, and that he loved his granddaughter.

And then there was the father who stood up with his son and daughter in front of the group. He hugged each of them as he said: "I love you." The daughter responded: "Daddy, I love you. I miss you. I want you to come home." Overcome with emotion, her father stated to the group: "Excuse me" as he, his daughter, and his son turned their backs to the group, huddled as they held on to each other, and silently wept.

At the end of the session, one of the co-facilitators sensed the need for the mood to be lightened and asked: "Who knows a joke that they can tell the group? Let's have one of the children tell a joke." The room erupted in laughter when one of the older children – a teenager – offered a humorous riddle.

The emergence of an armed corrections officer punctuated the fact that it was time for the session to end. She walked into the room, positioned herself against a wall, and stood silently as she observed the fathers and children hugging each other amid choruses of "I love you." Within seconds, the children and their fathers separated and moved to opposite ends of the room in front of a huge and thick metal door. Yet it seemed as if everyone was moving in slow motion. As the group of fathers and children silently moved to a respective door located at the far corner of the meeting room, they exchanged one final glance at each other before disappearing behind the door. No words were spoken. As the group of children silently moved through the door leading to a ramp that would reunite them with their mothers who were waiting in the prison lobby on the next floor, I looked back at the group of fathers who were exiting the meeting room. The group of men at the door had dwindled down to two. I watched the last two fathers in the group turn to glance at their children. These men never uttered a sound, but the somber look in their eyes spoke volumes as they took a last glimpse at their children before disappearing behind the metal door.

As the fathers returned to their cells, the children made their way up the winding ramp where they were met by a corrections officer stationed at an open metal door who escorted them to the huge reception area of the prison's lobby. Mothers and legal guardians participating in the FACT Experience Initiative had returned from their dinner meeting. The women talked with each other as they waited for their child to arrive in the lobby. After spending several hours with their fathers, the children were reunited with their mothers and legal guardians, who greeted them with smiles and hugs. As they walked out of the prison, a few mothers could be overheard asking: "How did it go with you and your father?"

Case Study

The father and child visitations that occur as a component of the FACT Experience Initiative provide fathers not only with time to bond with their child but also to talk to the child about any problems he or she is having that are brought to the father's attention. One father participating in the FACT Experience Initiative discovered that his son was having problems in school. He performed research that provided him with the name of the principal and address of his son's school. The father wrote a letter to the principal of his son's school that explained that he was an incarcerated father participating in the FACT Experience Initiative. He asked to receive a copy of his son's suspension letter, progress reports, report cards, and a general update on his son. He explained to the principal that he wanted to review the documents so that he could "help meet the school in the middle" to help resolve his son's issues that were impacting his behavior and academic performance. In his letter to the principal of his son's school, the incarcerated father also explained that after reviewing his son's school records, he would talk to his son to find out why he is having problems in school and work with his son to resolve the issues causing the problems. The principal responded to the incarcerated father's letter by providing him with all the information he asked for. And the principal thanked the incarcerated father for contacting him and stated that during his decade-long career, he had never received correspondence from an incarcerated parent asking for help to resolve a child's behavioral and academic issues. The incarcerated father shared the principal's response with members of U-CAN. As a result, members of U-CAN added another component to the FACT Experience Initiative. This component took the form of fathers writing to the principal of their child's school to request copies of his or her report card, progress reports, and any disciplinary reports.

The FACT Experience Initiative helped to establish a partnership between incarcerated fathers and their child's school. But the story does not end here. When the incarcerated father in question was released from prison in 2014, he attended an arranged meeting with the superintendent of the School District of Philadelphia. The meeting was the direct result of the partnership formed between the incarcerated father and his son's school. Upon learning about the development, the Philadelphia School District's superintendent not only agreed that incarcerated fathers should have a copy of their children's report cards and records but also stated he would advise all principals of schools throughout the School District of Philadelphia to provide incarcerated fathers, upon request, with a copy of their child's report cards and records. Before doing so, school principals would be required to contact the mother of the child to obtain her permission to have the records released to the child's incarcerated father. The father continues to play a proactive role in the life of his son. Since his father's return, the two of them continue to have a strong bond. The young man excels academically. He is an honor roll student and he is no longer bringing home suspension letters.

Another success story involves an incarcerated father who graduated from the FACT Initiative and was released from SCI Phoenix in 2015. He is raising his family with his wife who also participated and completed the FACT Experience Initiative. Shortly after his return to his family and community, the gentleman in question became the founder and executive director of a nonprofit organization. And he has become the first father graduating from the FACT Experience Initiative to successfully complete his parole!

The FACT Experience Initiative has not only helped incarcerated fathers establish bonds with their children and resolve any issues their child is experiencing, it has also helped to shape the policy of the school district in the nation's fifth largest metropolitan area – a policy that now allows incarcerated fathers to have access to their child's academic and disciplinary records, provided the mother of the child gives her written consent.

Lessons Learned

When one looks at the FACT Experience Initiative, the old adage "wisdom comes from all places" immediately comes to mind. A group of brilliant gentlemen, whom society has, for the most part, written off simply because they are incarcerated, has a deep-seated understanding of the irreparable damage that fatherlessness, intergenerational incarceration, and the school-to-prison pipeline wreaks upon families, communities, cities, and even a nation. They acted on that deep-seated understanding by designing a dynamic and results-oriented two-tiered parenting program with an embedded and powerful psychological component that equips incarcerated fathers and the mother and legal guardian of their children with parenting, co-parenting, and relationship-building skills.

From a practitioner's perspective, the FACT Experience Initiative demonstrates the critical need to bring incarcerated fathers to the table when designing parenting programs. Incarcerated fathers constitute a group of parents who are marginalized and have specific and unique needs. Most parenting programs have a "one-size-fits-all" design. I think it is important for me to say that I am not casting aspersions on the parenting programs that currently exist for incarcerated fathers. The parenting programs, resources, and support services currently available to incarcerated fathers are extremely helpful. As marginalized souls, incarcerated fathers, do not have one-size-fits-all issues. Let us go one step further. Incarcerated fathers are not the only marginalized souls. Their children and the mother of their children are also marginalized, and they, too, have specific and unique issues. Because incarcerated souls conceived the FACT Experience Initiative, it does not have a one-size-fits-all design. It is tailored to effectively address the specific and unique issues of marginalized parents – incarcerated fathers and the mothers and legal guardians of the children.

Conclusion

Positively shaping the minds and souls of our children is a very daunting task. For incarcerated fathers, this task is exacerbated by their set of circumstances. Yet if incarcerated fathers are provided with the necessary skills and tools that are tailored to address their specific and unique needs, they can and will transcend the obstacles created by their set of circumstances; develop a strong, loving, and nurturing relationship with their child; and help resolve any issues that their child is having at school or at home. As clearly demonstrated herein, it is not enough to provide incarcerated fathers with parenting, co-parenting, problem solving, and relationship skills and tools. The mothers and legal guardians of the children of incarcerated fathers must also be equipped with these same skills and tools and connected to any resources or support services they may need. The FACT Experience Initiative is a powerfully successful parenting program because it is designed *by* marginalized souls *for* marginalized souls.

What we have learned here is that the most effective parenting programs for incarcerated fathers are those that are holistically designed and implemented. We have also learned that the most effective and successful parenting programs for incarcerated fathers are designed by incarcerated souls. To that end, I am proposing that fatherhood practitioners and organizations seek out the counsel of incarcerated fathers regarding the design and implementation of parenting initiatives. I am further proposing that consideration be given to permitting incarcerated fathers serve on the advisory boards of fatherhood organizations and/or to act as consultants to fatherhood practitioners and organizations together with institutions that design and implement local, state, and national public policy that directly and indirectly impacts fathers and addresses their full and equal access to essential resources and support services.

References

Lee, D. (2001). The spiritual force. *In Search of Fatherhood®*, 3(1), 37–38.

Mural Arts Philadelphia. Retrieved from https://www.muralarts.org/artworks/fathers-and-children-together/.

Sawyer, W., & Wagner, P. (2020). *Mass incarceration: The whole pie 2020*. Prison Policy Institute. Retrieved from https://www.prisonpolicy.org/reports/pie2020.html.

6 Engaging and Working with African American Fathers in Schools

Tasha Alston

Introduction

African American fathers, regardless of class, do not have a "voice" within the literature on parental involvement. The marginalization and exclusion of African American fathers within the literature on parental involvement hinders the opportunity for authentic partnerships to occur. The limited inclusion of African American fathers is problematic considering parental involvement affects academic achievement and African American students continue to underperform academically (Epstein, 2013; Jeynes, 2005; Reynolds, Howard, & Jones, 2013).

Lamb, Pleck, Charnov, and Levine (1985) created a staple conceptualization of father involvement that explains father involvement as a father's interaction, availability, and responsibility for his children. Interaction is the extent of the father's direct contact with the child; availability is the fathers' potential availability for interaction by being present and accessible to his child whether or not direct interaction is occurring; responsibility is the role fathers take to make sure their child is taken care of and resources are provided. African American fathers and father figures are involved in and play an important role in the lives of their children (Abel, 2012; Fagan, 2000; Lamb, 1987). They also contribute to the personal and educational growth and development their children experience.

However, a significant portion of the literature on parental involvement continuously refers to African American fathers from a deficient perspective. In fact, Boyd-Franklin (2003) stated this deficient perspective consistently portrays African American fathers as absent, missing, peripheral, and not involved in their children's personal and educational lives. According to Hutchinson (1996), this deficient portrayal and negative imagery of African American males works towards the assassination of their image and perpetuates stereotypes that have existed about African American males for decades in American society. Unfortunately, this deficient perspective pushes African American fathers to the margins of the literature on parental involvement and diminishes the involvement that African American fathers have in their children's education. This marginalization silences African American fathers and makes African American fathers invisible within the social science literature. This deficient perspective of African American fathers hinders researchers' and educators' ability to see or understand the contributions that African American fathers make in their children's personal and educational lives.

Although African American fathers are overwhelmingly referred to from a deficient perspective and largely portrayed as missing and not involved, these fathers are involved and want to be more involved in their children's personal and educational lives (Coles & Green, 2010; Connor & White, 2011; Grantham & Henfield, 2011). In fact, McFadden, Tamis-LeMonda, and Cabrera (2011) posited African American fathers are more involved in their children's lives than are White and Latino fathers. McFadden et al. (2011) stated:

> In comparison to White children, about twice as many Hispanic children and six times as many Black children live in households without a resident father; yet among this group of children who do not live with their fathers, nearly all Black children have some contact with their fathers (94%) whereas children's rate of contact with non-resident fathers are lower are somewhat lower among White and Hispanic children (82% and 79%, respectively). (p. 121)

According to McFadden et al. (2011), African American fathers are involved in their children's personal and educational lives in different ways and to different degrees. African American fathers may not be involved in traditional ways that researchers and educators expect. However, Lareau (1987) stated the involvement that African American families, including African American fathers, have and the contributions that they make in their children's personal and educational lives are still important.

In a similar vein, Allen (2012) stated that African American fathers contribute and are involved by intervening and drawing upon their cultural wealth to help their African American sons divert school-based racial micro-aggressions and the potential negative outcomes of school racism. According to Allen (2012) racial micro-aggressions are the subtle, stunning, automatic, nonverbal exchanges that are put-downs of African Americans by offenders, and cultural wealth is a form of cultural capital people of color draw upon to fight discrimination. African American fathers utilized social capital and navigational capital to help their sons divert racial micro-aggressions and school-based racism. Social capital refers to networks of people and community resources that allow people of color to succeed inside and outside of their communities (Allen, 2012). Navigational capital refers to the ability to maneuver through institutions that were not fully intended for the inclusion of people of color (Allen, 2012).

African American fathers were also involved in culturally specific ways by socializing their sons to prepare for issues of race and racial micro-aggressions within the school environment and teaching their sons how to navigate racial micro-aggressions within the school environment.

Abel (2012) examined African American fathers' involvement in the school-based lives of their elementary school-age children using the Hoover-Dempsey and Sandler model of parent involvement and Epstein's framework of involvement. Abel (2012) administered a demographic form, a revised Hoover-Dempsey and Sandler model of the parental involvement process, and Epstein and Clark Salinas's questionnaires for teacher and parent in elementary and middle grades. Results revealed significant findings related to invitations from others and home–school communication, fathers' life context and school-based parental involvement, and fathers' life context and invitations from others. Abel (2012) displayed the importance of understanding factors that affect African American fathers' decisions to be involved in their children's learning and understanding how African American fathers choose to be involved.

If researchers and educators are interested in partnering with African American fathers to provide their children with additional support to enhance academic achievement, then African American fathers must be included in the discussion. It is imperative for researchers and educators to bring African American fathers to "the table" and to begin to listen to the "voice" of African American fathers to understand how African American fathers are and want to be involved. Obtaining an increased understanding of the perspectives of involvement that African American fathers have will benefit authentic partnerships with African American fathers.

The purpose of this chapter is to show how narrative can be utilized as a culturally relevant method with critical race theory (CRT) to privilege the "voice" of African American fathers to better understand the involvement that African American fathers have in their children's education and engage them further.

Practice

CRT begins with the notion that racism is a normal part of American society (Bell, 1995; Ladson-Billings, 1998). CRT asserts racism is so enmeshed in the fabric of American society that it appears normal. CRT has six foundational tenets that include racism is a normal part of American society; CRT expresses skepticism towards dominant legal claims of neutrality, objectivity, colorblindness, and meritocracy; CRT challenges ahistoricism and insists on a contextual/historical analysis of the law; CRT insists on the recognition of the experiential knowledge of people of color; CRT is interdisciplinary and takes into account the intersectionality of various forms of subordination and oppression (e.g., race, class, gender); and CRT works towards the elimination of racial oppression as a part of the larger goal of ending all forms of oppression (Dixson & Rousseau, 2005).

Calmore (as cited in Tate, 1997) stated:

> Critical race theory challenges the universality of White experience/
> judgment as the authoritative standard that binds people of color and
> normatively measures, directs, controls, and regulates the terms of
> proper thought, expression, presentation, and behavior. As represented
> by legal scholars, critical race theory challenges the dominant discourse
> on race and racism. (pp. 196–197)

According to Ladson-Billings and Tate (1995) "voice," or naming one's own
reality, is also a theme of CRT. Critical race theorists revere parables,
chronicles, stories, counterstories, poetry, fiction, and revisionist histories.
CRT departs from mainstream scholarship by focusing on the experiential
knowledge of people of color (Ladson-Billings, 1998), and CRT recognizes
that the experiential knowledge of people of color is legitimate, appropriate,
and critical to understanding race (Solorzano & Yasso, 2001) and how race
operates and permutes to affect the lives of people of color (Ladson-Billings &
Donnor, 2005). CRT permits researchers to privilege the "voice" of people
of color to hear the counterstories of people of color, specifically the counterstories of African American fathers. According to Delgado (1995), counterstories are stories that "counter" or act to deconstruct the dominant or
master narrative and present another side to the dominant discourse (Milner
IV, 2012; Solorzano & Yasso, 2002; Tate IV, 1997). Counterstories go against
the established order and control (Berry III, Thunder, & McClain, 2011).
Counterstories are critical of the master narrative and come out of the experiences of individuals from marginalized groups whose voice, perspective,
and consciousness have been suppressed and devalued (Bell, 1995; Berry III
et al., 2011; Delgado, 1995; Solorzano & Yasso, 2002).

CRT allowed the researcher to partner with African American fathers to
hear their counterstories and to utilize their "voice" to understand how
African American fathers are involved in their children's education. CRT
also permitted the researcher to collaborate with African American fathers
to construct a sense of human agency to support their African American
children with academic achievement (Ladson-Billings & Donnor, 2005) for
the betterment of society as a whole. These stories and counterstories were
obtained by interviewing individuals that self-identify as African American
males and as being the father of a school-age child. A narrative method
allowed the researcher to obtain detailed stories and counterstories (Bruner,
1990; Bruner, 2004; Chase, 2005) of African American fathers to better
understand the involvement that African American fathers have in their
children's education. According to Clandinin and Connelly (2000):

> Narrative inquiry is a way of understanding experiences. It is collabora-
> tion between researcher and participants, over time, in a place, or series
> of places, and in social interaction with milieus. An inquirer enters the

> matrix in the midst and progresses in this same spirit, concluding the inquiry still in the midst of living and telling, reliving and retelling, the stories of the experiences that make up people's lives, both individual and social...narrative inquiry is stories lived and told. (p. 20)

Narrative connects to a foundational tenet of CRT that focuses on the experiential knowledge of people of color. Narrative permitted the researcher to honor, value, and recognize the experiential knowledge that African American fathers have while simultaneously viewing this experiential knowledge as having the potential to contribute to new knowledge (Solorzano & Yasso, 2001).

Case Study

African American fathers of children in kindergarten through twelfth grade were purposively selected and interviewed for 60–90 minutes. The following criteria were set for participants because these characteristics aligned with the purpose of the research: (1) self-identify as African American, (2) 21 years of age or older, and (3) father of school-age (K–12) child. It is also important to note that it appeared the African American males within the African American community that referred or nominated fathers for the study also set a sub-criteria for the fathers they chose to refer or nominate to the study. These sub-criteria appeared to include being a father who is actively involved in their children's education. As a result, all of the participants were African American fathers who were actively involved in their children's education.

Community nomination was used to select participants through direct contact with the African American community (Foster, 1990). According to Foster (1990) community nomination means participants were chosen by direct contact with the African American community.

The researcher identified potential African American fathers to participate in the study by visiting the African American community and African American community organizations (through organizations such as barbershops, churches, and community organizations where African American fathers congregate); posting flyers with research contact information for individuals interested in participating in the study; explaining the purpose of the study to African American males within the African American community; and verbally informing African American males and other individuals within the African American community about the study.

Description of Participants

Four African American fathers who live in the southeastern region of the United States agreed to participate in the interview, and each was given a pseudonym to protect his identity. Participant D was a 47-year-old African American male educated at the bachelor's level with two children ages 16 and 22. Participant D

Table 6.1 Participant Demographic Chart

Participant	Age of Children	Education	Participant Age
D	16	MA	47
P	16, 20, 24	PhD(c)	42
G	12, 15	MBA	45
C	7, 8, 9, 10	HS/Trade	45

Key
HS/Trade = High School and trade school
MBA = Master of Business Administration
MA = Master's degree
PhD(c) = Doctoral candidate

is the owner of a barbershop in the southeastern region of the United States. The researcher met participant D at the barbershop to conduct the interview at the close of the business day. Participant D informed the researcher that his own father was involved in his personal and educational life when participant D was an elementary, middle, and high school student. Participant D also informed the researcher that he is a resident father as he resides in the home with his child.

Participant P was a 42-year-old African American father educated at the doctoral level with three children ages 16, 20, and 24. Participant P was a healthcare executive. The researcher met Participant P at a healthcare organization at the close of the business day. Participant P also informed the researcher that his own father was involved in his personal and educational life when participant P was an elementary, middle, and high school student. Participant P is a resident and nonresident father as he resides with his youngest daughter and his oldest children live with him for half of the week.

Participant G is a 45-year-old African American father educated at the master's level with two children ages 15 and 12. Participant G was the owner of a transportation company. The researcher met participant G at a local location in the southeastern region of the United States at the close of the business day. Participant G informed the researcher that his biological father was not involved in his life, but his uncle (Participant G's uncle is Participant's G's mother's brother) took responsibility to be his father figure and was involved during his elementary, middle, high school, and college education. Participant G is a resident father and resides in the home with his children.

Participant C is a 45-year-old African American father educated at the high school level with a trade in barbering with four children ages 10, 9, 8, and 7. Participant C is the owner of a nonprofit organization that teaches inner city children how to play chess. The researcher met Participant C at a local community center where the chess program takes place after business hours. Participant C informed the researcher that he grew up in a group home and as a result he did not have a father involved in his life. Participant

C informed the researcher that the pastor from the church that he attended as a youth served as his father figure. Participant C informed the researcher that his pastor was involved in his high school education. Participant C is a resident father as he resides in the home with his children.

Lessons Learned

The fathers' narratives revealed the following themes: (1) Involved in Education: A priority and legacy; (2) Inside Out: African American fathers are involved in their children's education in the home environment and outside of the school environment – teaching; guiding and training; providing; modeling; and encouragement, motivation, and psychological support; and (3) Attributes for Academic Achievement: Strategy and characteristics.

1   *Involved in Education: A priority and legacy (they can't take education away from you)*

African American fathers value education and perceive education as an utmost priority. African American fathers are committed to ensuring their children become educated because education is a utility vehicle that will affect their future quality of life. Therefore, African American fathers are involved and committed to ensuring their children also view education as a priority.

African American fathers' perception of education as a priority stems from a multigenerational perspective. Specifically, elders in African American fathers' families and previous generations (e.g., mothers, fathers, grandmother, aunts, uncle, cousins, father figures, neighbors, etc.) taught them about the importance of education for African American families and African American communities. The importance of education as a priority and legacy is passed down in African American fathers' families from generation to generation (Hattery & Smith, 2007). Participant D told a story and explained the legacy of education passed on from his grandmother and other family members. Participant D captured education as a priority and legacy poignantly:

> I looked at education as the highest top and as the utmost because as I said, my mother, um, ya know was a college graduate and my aunt who was a year older than her went to college. It was drilled in us from my grandmother. And as I said, my mother and her friends and cousins, they were teachers in my town. And they really took their experiences from when they went to college and transferred that to us as young people. Then also with my grandmother from the story that came about when my mother was graduating from high school in 1965, my grandmother worked in a White person's kitchen, a lady's

kitchen, and the lady asked, what is your daughter going to do when she graduates? And my grandmother answered, she is going to college, and the lady said, NO, there is a lady across the street on the street over that needs someone to work in her kitchen. And my grandmother said, NO, I don't want her to do that. So the white woman said, if you do that I am going to cut off your aid. So my grandmother said, you do what you gotta do, but my daughter is going to college.

My mother went to college, as a result, my aunt went to college the next year, me and my brother and my sister went to college also and graduated and finished. Um, so I mean education is, I am always looking at it as paramount, FIRST, if you perceive that as my grandmother would say "They can't take that from you." Yes, so I look at education from a positive standpoint. I always carried my books with me. I still have a book bag of books right now, matter fact I got two.

One here in the shop and one outside. And I got a gang of books even in the back of the barbershop. At my house, I keep em, I go to the thrift store, so I am always, it's a continuum of education. I might not be in a professional setting or school, what have you, but I think learning is, you should be doing that on a continuum.

Participant D's narrative showed how education is a priority from generation to generation; education was a priority in the era of racial segregation and remains a priority for the current generation. Each generation understood the importance, value, and utility that education offered, and each generation remained committed to becoming educated as a result of understanding the experiences that previous generations had to go through in order to obtain an education.

Participant G also similarly spoke to education as a priority and the legacy of education passed from generation to generation within his family. Participant G stated that his mother, uncle (who he referred to as his father figure), and aunts continuously taught him from the time that he was a small child that education is a priority and the key to success in life. Participant G succinctly stated each generation was taught:

That education is the key to success, and the more education you have, the better prepared you will be in life.

Participant G stated that his uncle, who acted as a father figure throughout his life, taught him about the importance of education as a priority and also passed on the legacy of education to him. Participant G captured his uncle's involvement in teaching him education is a priority and how his uncle also passed on the legacy of education to him:

Whole influence. He took all of the responsibility for me. He made sure that I was fully educated. He made sure that I graduated from high school. He made sure that I want to college. He made sure I got a bachelor's degree. He made sure I got a master's degree. He was very influential in all aspects of my education. Financially, socially, totally.

Participant P and Participant C also expressed similar sentiments connected to education as a priority and legacy. For example, Participant P stated that his mother attended college but was unable to graduate as a result of life circumstances. As a result, Participant P's mother was adamant about ensuring that her children received their college education.

Participant C stated that although he grew up in a group home, his pastor served as a father figure and his pastor ensured that he focused on getting a trade or an education and ensuring that he also made sure that when he had children they would also become educated.

Each participant's narrative tells of the importance of education as a priority within his family and of education being passed on as a legacy from generation to generation. Furthermore, the narratives display the collective approach that takes place within the African American community to ensure that all children are taught to understand the value of education. This collective approach involves families, kinship family members, teachers, friends, and community members working together to instill the value of education and to ensure that each child within each generation becomes educated.

2   *Inside Out: African American fathers are involved in their children's education outside of the school environment: guiding and training; providing; teaching; modeling; encouragement, motivation, and psychological support.*

The narratives (counterstories) of African American fathers reveal that African American fathers are intricately involved in their children's education outside of the school environment by guiding and training their children, providing, teaching their children, acting as models for their children and by giving encouragement, motivation, and psychological support.

Guiding and Training

African American fathers are involved outside of the school environment by providing their children with guidance and training to achieve academically. African American fathers correlate academic achievement with enhanced quality of life outcomes and future success. As a result, African American fathers utilize their experiential knowledge to consistently guide their children towards academic achievement. African American fathers guide and train their children to work towards academic achievement on a continuous basis. Participant D succinctly tells how he provided guidance:

So, ya know me as being as somewhat, like I said the manager, not ya know the technician, like my wife is a technician, she is a teacher and she knows all the lingo, I stand back and I assess maybe from a manager standpoint or visionary standpoint, to see if what he is doing is applicable of him moving toward the greater vision of him with the degree and the career that's, ya know, productive. And I am always asking input from teachers and different professionals that come in, what are the latest trends, what is going on, what is taking place in your career, and what should my son be doing, what classes should he be taking? What emphasis should he be looking at, what focus should he be having? And then I kinda curtail and customize, and see, and put him in a direction to make sure that the classes coincide with that and what's going on now.

Participant D tells how African American fathers train their children on a consistent basis throughout the child's life to ensure that the child is consistently working towards academic achievement. Once the child is trained to consistently work towards academic achievement, then this same training can be applied throughout other areas of life to enhance academic and life success. Participant D succinctly stated:

Oh yes, by design. Yes, because it is to be modeled in college and on the next level. To be independent, and to be able to go in and pursue your goals and tasks. When no one else will and we are not there. Yes, most definitely, that is one of the actual goals is to be very independent. Yes.

Participant D explained African American fathers also intentionally activate their social capital to better guide and train their child to achieve academically:

I talk with my clients who are in education and in high school and college education and I ask them what is needed now? Where is education going, and then I also ask them what can he be reading, what should he be doing, what programs should he be involved in? What is needed now, where is the shift, where is education going? What tools do you all use now? Like, I found out from a high school as well as college that now children can upload all their assignments into their portfolio on the internet and that's how they are graded and that can also be used if you are going to later on do an internship and you can send the portfolio and also tell a potential employer, hey I am doing this as well as college. You send that and a lot more things are digital now and that's what I am finding.

When I find out different things, what I end up doing is instead of waiting till I get home, so I do not forget it, I end up sending text messages or e-mail to him and his mother. Because I am on the frontline getting this information. In the networking sharing forum right here in this barbershop. And I will take time out, and sometimes my clients will get mad with me because I am asking questions, standing and cutting with clippers, and I am listening, and I am absorbing and taking notes mentally, and as soon as that client leaves, I text it or e mail it out and send it to my wife and son.

Participant D's narrative tells how African American fathers utilize non-traditional forms of involvement outside of the school environment to guide and train their children with skills that enhance academic achievement outside and inside of the school environment.

African American fathers also understand the importance of guiding and training their children consistently from an early age to help solidify the foundation for academic achievement and life success. Participant D poignantly summarized African American fathers' purpose behind guiding and training their children. Participant D stated:

If you want the next direction to excel and outperform you, then you have to provide them with direction. You have to have a base and foundation for them to build on; I think it's important for each generation to have a foundation to build on that is concrete, substantial, significant, and purposeful. It can't be fragmented. You really have to have a blueprint for success for which they can build on and add to. That is why I am involved.

Providing

The narratives of African American fathers reveal African American fathers are involved in their children's education by providing. African American fathers provide financial, educational, and cultural resources that support academic achievement and provide access to opportunities that enhance learning. African American fathers provide to decrease the barriers that children may experience as a result of not having access to financial, educational, and cultural resources as a result of the storied racial and historical context that exists and persists in American society that tremendously negatively affects people of color.

Participant P stated that when African American fathers provide financially, then this financial provision creates stability and this stability supports children's access to educational opportunities:

With fathers out of the home, it's more so financial that your voice is really heard through financial. When I say that, I mean that if you do not make sure that the kid is financially stable, then that is a whole nother issue. So if you are not financially stable, then the educational background is not going to be as stable because they are not going to have the opportunity to pursue any of these advanced things in life.

Showing the love and support and stability. I think that's very key, even if it's just love and support kids need the financial stability. I have just always been very big on that, because I think that's one of the things that can handicap kids is the financial stability. If they don't have that, then it's kinds hard for them. That mean they gotta work extra hard. And I think that over the years I have done an excellent job just kinda making sure they were financially able to participate in things that will encourage them, to give them opportunity.

Participant G also told how African American fathers are involved in ways that do not require finances and are still equally important by providing their children with educational resources to support academic achievement. Participant G provided his children with tutoring as an educational resource to help enhance academic achievement:

I actually have study sessions with them. Tutorials. I also go on their website with them to research what they need to do. I also help them with projects. I help them study. I help them do reports. I am literally involved in their weekly activities when it comes to their academics.

Participant C explained that he provides the education that his children receive because he homeschools his children. Participant C explained that he chose to provide his children with education through homeschooling because he felt the education that his children received in public school was inadequate:

I visited a private school and they had 5 or 6 students in a class, and I realize they can do better because with 5 or 6 students you can't help but do better. So, I realized that I can do the same thing and I will do better because that's my child. I took a class and it taught me how to be a better advocate for my child. And my wife was another one, she was like no. She wanted to homeschool from the get-go. If you look at the statistics for homeschooling, you will see it's rising if people knew they had the power to do so.

Participant D also referred to African American fathers providing for their children and posits that African American fathers provide for their children because African American fathers want their children to achieve academically and to have the best and be the best they can be in life. African American fathers understand the importance of ensuring their children have the necessary provisions to achieve academically. As a result, African

American fathers do what is necessary to provide for their children on a continuous basis.

Teaching

The narratives of African American fathers tell how African American fathers are involved in their children's education by teaching their children the importance of academic achievement and by teaching their children that education is a tool to be practically applied to help them achieve enhanced future quality of life outcomes and life goals. Stated differently, African American fathers correlate education and academic achievement with their children's ability to solve problems and gain future independence through the practical application of education. Participant D captured this sentiment:

> Academic achievement, what it looks like to me. What academic achievement looks like to me is progressive realization of one's goals. And that is determined through whatever a person deems is success in their eyes and them having that pursuit to realize those goals. And they can be lofty, they can be marginal, but success is in education, is in getting the comprehension of the information and being able to later on articulate that. So it's more than just, you have taken the class and got a good grade. Now it's, can you articulate that and apply it in a problem-solving scenario, whereby you can bring solutions to you know, the unit, the company, your business, the client. That is essential in this day and time. You know, the higher the mark, the better, but I think going forward, people are looking for people that can bring solutions that are applicable.

Participant G also posited education is a continuous process and education must be applicable in all aspects of life. As a result, he also teaches his children to be continuous learners and to be able to apply what is learned in all aspects of life:

> I look at schooling as a continuous process. Schooling never changes because the environment is ever changing, the landscaping is always changing, computer programming is always changing, technology is always changing, so you have to be a continuous learner and you have to be cognizant of that.

Participant C stated that homeschooling allows him to teach his children and to understand his children's gifts so they can apply those gifts to greatness. Participant C stated he attempts to cater some of his children's education to their gifts so that they can apply their gifts within their education:

At home I can see what gifts my child has, and I can cater the education to those gifts so they can apply them. And we focus on you being okay. Being better and making higher. If I know my child is having a challenge, I can put him into something to help build him. Homeschooling helps me to help them excel to where they can use their gifts, to where they can be great.

Participant P also referred to the importance of teaching children so that they understand the importance of education, of academic achievement, and of following through and completing and achieving educational and life goals they set out to accomplish.

Modeling

African American fathers are involved in their children's education by modeling actions that will help their children to achieve academically. African American fathers continuously model educational attainment and learning. The African American fathers interviewed explained that it was important for them to obtain an education not only because it was instilled in them by previous generations, but also because they are models (an exemplar) for their children to achieve academically. Participant D stated that he is college educated and continues to read to enhance learning because he understands that he is a model for his son:

I graduated from college. College degree in accounting. B.A. Most definitely, I read. He sees me reading. Ya know, I look at the news. I look at 60 Minutes. I even have him look at 60 Minutes. The debates that we have on TV now between Democrats and Republican, he is required to look at those and to give a synopsis on those. Sometimes even different financial things that come on CNBC, so we even have a discussion about those. Even I have an investment club. So I have shown him how to analyze stock, look for stock, find stock, and to give me his report, a two-page report on those. So I think this could come back to some of the things we were talking about that did not come to mind before, so yes, we have a monthly meeting for the investment club where we review one to two stocks per month, so he is required to come to one or two of those out of the month and to give us his report.

He also gives us his opinion on should we do a manual educational study of stocks on version or if we should so an online tutorial version. He thought the online tutorial version would be a better way to go because it was more user friendly. So and that was in his 8th or 9th grade year. So, yes, he sees me reading and doing financial things, so I have books that I read and I read those and if I have him also sometimes go back and reread something that I have read. And you tell my reading because it's highlighted in red, underlines with a pencil, bracketed and it might be an ear pinch on the page, so he knows when I see something in the reading that's important.

Participant P stated that despite the challenges of having a child at an early age that he also worked hard throughout the years to receive his education and to model the expectation of education, academic achievement and following through and achieving goals for his son:

> Yes, I think that when I went back to finish school about 13 years ago. So that really changed my whole perspective. But it was showing that I had completions in my life. Before that I just had college credits. I was just a high school graduate. And that's how I had to look at it, no matter how many college credits I had, I was just a high school graduate. So that really changed the whole perspective of my life. And to fast forward to finish my master's, it really solidified where I was going as far as career wise. I had the working career, but I had to understand how to verbalize it. And now I have advanced through career opportunities, self-employment opportunities, to a doctoral degree.

> Yes, I felt like I grew up with my son. I was 20. Let's see, he is 25 so we kinda grown up together. So it's kinda like he can look at me and say, okay, Dad I have seen you do it, I have been by your side, he has grown up seeing me do it, so I kinda been by your side. And that's how I look at him. It's like, you're not just my son, it's like I grew up with you. And I groomed you to do these things. So I know you can do it. And that's the thing, never accepting that no I can't do it. Figure out a way to do it. So I think it's been great, him seeing me through the struggle years, seeing me accomplish things, so that has been great for him.

Participant G similarly stated that he realizes that he is a model for his children. Participant G models hard work doing and his best on a continuous basis so that his children understand that hard work and doing your best leads to success. As a result, Participant G continuously teaches his children of the importance of applying hard work, applying your best at all times, and learning coursework so that coursework can be applied in a practical way to support life success. Participant G succinctly stated:

> To do your best was highly recommended, but to do as much as you could do. Not always getting the perfect score. It was about do as well as you can do. Take the time. Learn the coursework and do what you need to do to achieve your goals.

I have always been on the side of doing your best. That's the only way you can be successful. You can't be successful by doing half the work. You have to do all of the work and some and extra.

Participant C stated that he models utilizing your education to support entrepreneurship so that his children understand the importance of utilizing education to create ownership. Participant C posited that when he shows his children how education can help them to be entrepreneurs, then it motivates them to achieve academically:

I try to teach my children to use what they have to be self-sufficient. That it's not intelligent to have an education and to not use that education to create something for themselves. If he has to put in applications and work for somebody else to make him feel successful and get a big paycheck because at the end of the day it comes back to that common denominator, I need another job. Work for yourself with all this education I have. Don't live to work and retire off of what somebody else created. Education is great if it's used. I got that from barbering school, and I show them that through what I do.

Encouragement, Motivation, and Psychological Support

The African American fathers who were interviewed understand their children will face barriers as they work towards academic achievement. As a result, African American fathers also understand the importance of providing their children with encouragement, motivation, and psychological support to help their children overcome barriers and to help their children have the resilience needed to continue to work towards academic achievement in the face of these barriers. Participant D captured this involvement and explained how he was involved by encouraging, motivating, and providing his child with psychological support to help his child with overcoming an academic setback:

I mean there was a time recently where he did something, and he thought we were going to be mad. And we were at first, and he was down on himself and then a week or so went by and he was still upset. I told him, look, in life you are going to make mistakes, the thing about that is if you keep hitting yourself in the head about your mistakes then you are not going to achieve anything, you have to get back up and swing the bat the next three out of ten times. An older gentleman who works in baseball told me. Do you realize that you can go to the baseball hall of fame if you just hit three out of ten balls and get on base three times out of ten? I relate that to my son. That you are going to strike out seven times, but it's the three that you hit, and you will go to the hall of fame, so life is very similar. You have to keep getting up and you will have more failures then success, but you have to keep shooting for those successes.

Participant G similarly stated that he also involved daily by proving his children with motivation, encouragement, and psychological support. Participant G stated that he attempts to encourage and motivate his children when they are right but also when they are wrong so that they attempt to improve in the area of wrongdoing and so that they will be motivated to do better each time:

I try to help them on a daily basis. So, if I am encouraging them I am making sure that it is not only the good that I am encouraging but the bad also. If they do bad in something, then I encourage them that you can do better, just focus on the next time and you will do better, you will achieve your goals.

Participant C similarly stated:

With the way I grew up, I let my children know that they have my support, know that they can depend on me, know that they have someone, because I want what's best for them.

The African American fathers within this study understand the importance of providing their children with motivation, encouragement, and psychological support to help them achieve academically but also to help them understand that they have to have resilience and tenacity throughout life to overcome challenges and to persist in the face of challenges. As a result, African American fathers encourage their children and provide them with motivation to help them get through challenges and to help them understand that although you may not always be successful, if you continue on in the face of challenges, then eventually you will obtain your educational and personal goals.

3   *Attributes for Academic Achievement: Strategy and Characteristics*

African American fathers attribute the academic achievement their children experience to being strategic and having key characteristics. These key characteristics include hard work, critical thinking, persistence, a commitment to excellence, doing your best at all times, and visualizing your goals and future. African American fathers are involved by translating these characteristics and teaching their children that these key characteristics will help them to achieve academically and to be successful later in life. Participant D stated:

I understand the importance and the significance of studying hard, and being diligent, and a commitment to excellence. To succeed in a global economy. And doing so, I can't translate that to him and he thinks that

I am somewhat going overboard, but I think that in due time he will see the need and value in what I am ordering.

Participant D also explained how he teaches his son to think critically about education and ensuring the education he receives coincides with his future vision and goals. Participant D tells his son a story and utilizes the story to help his son understand the importance of thinking critically about education and ensuring his education strategically coincides with future goals:

> I tell him that education is important, but you have to, you can't just take a bunch of classes, like one of my roommates did. Come to find out and he said that he was inspired by me when I went to college, I said to him, you should be finished with your degree by now, and he said, at a college, I have actually taken more classes then I need for a degree, but I can't get a degree because I never declared a major, and as a result, he said I never took classes grouped together to result in a major. I use that analogy and I tell my son to take classes, get educated, and to keep the end in mind and see where this class and information coincides with the end in mind. And how it drives you there and how it pushes you there and how it propels you there. Education is important, but it has to be relative to something that you are trying to achieve. A goal, it could be a house, or retirement or a better career or a business, so it has to be applicable to be marketable.

Participant D also attributes academic achievement to having a vision, thinking critically about direction, and being strategic. Participant D understands having a vision, working hard towards that vision and strategy, may help increase the chance of success, and as a result he explains that he teaches his son to always have a vison, work hard, and think critically to achieve academically and to obtain life goals. Participant D also posited that he embraces these characteristics as his own mission so that he can model them for his son and support his son with achievement:

> Number one you have to be a visionary. You have to first embrace looking out at the landscape and envisioning where you are going in ten to fifteen years. And then back into what it takes to get there. Somewhat like a movie, you have to envision the end of the movie. And figure out what props, what people, what tools, what computers, what equipment all that is needed to get there, that is the technical side of it. Then you have to be a producer or manager and figure out how to coordinate all these things. But it first starts with being a visionary, you gotta be a visionary and look long-term range and find out where is society going and where have we evolved from as well.

So as a parent, as a father, as a father especially, you really have to embrace the quality of being a visionary as your concept or mission.

Participant P similarly attributed academic achievement to key characteristics. Participant P states that you have to take initiative and have the drive to propel you towardsuccess: Participant P stated "You got to get up and make it happen."

Participant P also attributed academic achievement to persistence and commitment. Participant P stated that having persistence, commitment, and the will to accomplish helps individuals to follow through with goal completion and also helps individuals to finish what is started. Participant P stated he teaches his children these characteristics because he understands these characteristics will help them to achieve academically and in life:

One of the key things is that I want him to accomplish. Accomplish what you started. I don't want him to look back ten years from now and have any incompletes in his life. Because even with him moving forward in life, a completion of what you started in life helps you educational wise. It helps you personally, it helps your endeavors to say, well, I can do it. It can help you start your own business. And because if you have a history of incompletes in your life, it means that everything that you start you are not going to finish. So that's how I feel. It's a recognition of completion.

Participant G also attributes academic achievement to key characteristics that include discipline, organization, analytical skills, and being honest with oneself:

Discipline, organization, analyzing the situation, and figuring out exactly what should and should not happen. Learning to be honest with oneself. Knowing you need help. Don't try to do something on your own and feel as if you can't ask someone for help out with the situation. So I encourage them to ask for help if they ever get stumped on a situation.

Participant C attributed academic achievement to doing well for the sake of doing well:

Do well for the sake of doing well. You want to do well because you can do well.

The narratives of participants D, P, G, and C collectively tell us that African American fathers attribute academic achievement to key characteristics. These fathers also believe these characteristics will transfer to help their children with being successful later in life.

Privileging the voice of African American fathers challenges the deficient narrative that exists related to African American fathers throughout American society by showing the involvement that African American fathers have in their children's personal and educational lives. Of importance, privileging the voice of African American fathers brings African American fathers inside the margins of education. Privileging the voice of African American fathers also values, validates, and respects the diverse forms of involvement that African American fathers have in their children's personal and educational lives, especially the involvement that African American fathers have outside of the school environment.

The counterstories of African American fathers inform researchers, educators, administrators, practitioners, and policymakers that African American fathers are involved and want to be involved in their African American children's personal and educational lives. Without a doubt, African American fathers are committed to their role as fathers, committed to their children and families, and committed to being involved as partners in education to support their children with academic achievement and school success. African American fathers are an overlooked resource, and African American fathers are dynamic partners in education.

Although the research and literature on African American fathers is improving, there still remains a dearth of research and literature on African American fathers and on African American fathers' involvement in education. As a result, more research and literature is needed that privileges the voice of African American fathers; focuses directly on African American fathers to better understand the perceptions of African American fathers; and honors, values, validates, and respects the lived realities of African American fathers. More research is needed that partners with African American fathers as partners in education to support the academic achievement their African American children experience. More research is needed in partnership with African American fathers that utilizes culturally relevant theoretical frameworks and culturally relevant methodologies that permit the researcher to value, validate, and respect the experiential knowledge that African American fathers have.

More research is needed that places race in the forefront of the research to respect the full identities and experiences of African American fathers and African American males. African American fathers are an invaluable resource in education. It is time for American society to value and acknowledge the contributions that African American fathers and African American males make in the lives of their children, their families, their communities, and society for the betterment of society as a whole.

Conclusions

This study purposefully privileges the voices of African American fathers to understand the counterstories of African American fathers. Counterstories are stories that challenge the master deficient narrative; counterstories privilege and give voice to African American fathers to understand the involvement that African American fathers have in their children's lives. The counterstories within this study work to challenge the master deficient narrative and to change the narrative about African American fathers, and African American males.

The counterstories of African American fathers within this study reflect an accurate portrayal and depiction of African American fathers. African American fathers are dynamic. African American fathers play an important role in the lives of their children, families, and communities. African American fathers and African American males positively contribute to American society. African American fathers persist, persevere, and display tenacity to be successful in spite of the challenges they are faced with in American society. Without a doubt, significant amounts of the challenges that African American fathers and African American males are faced with in American society are related to context: racial context, historical context, social context, and political context. Without a doubt, context matters in the lives of African American fathers, and context must be considered when work of any kind is completed with African American fathers and African American males.

African American fathers have knowledge, including experiential knowledge, that can contribute to the creation of new knowledge. The voice of African American fathers informs researchers, administrators, educators, policymakers, and practitioners that African American fathers contribute to American society. African American fathers are engaged and involved in their children's personal and educational lives – and want to be engaged and involved. African American fathers and African American males are brilliant beyond measure, and the brilliance of African American fathers and African American males cannot be dimmed. African American fathers are a true source of pride for their children, families, and communities. African American fathers play a powerful role in their children's personal and educational lives. This narrative is an accurate portrayal and depiction of African American fathers and African American males throughout American society. This accurate portrayal of African American fathers and African American males' challenges and changes the master narrative. This narrative implores researchers, policymakers, administrators, educators, and practitioners to more closely the examine the narratives and stories that exist as it relates to African American fathers and African American males in American society. Of importance, the stories and counterstories (stories that challenge or counter the master narrative) of African American fathers compel researchers to ask the questions of whose stories are dominant, and whose voice is marginalized or silenced. Although the research is improving, the voice of African American fathers is all too often marginalized, muted, or silenced.

This research seeks to give voice to African American fathers and to bring African American fathers inside the margins of education, as partners in education. The "counterstories" of African American fathers inform researchers, educators, policymakers, administrators, and practitioners that African American fathers are dynamic partners in education.

Acknowledgments

This research did not receive any specific grant from funding agencies in the public, commercial, or not-for-profit sectors. The author would like to thank and acknowledge the African American fathers that participated in this study. The African American fathers within this study provided their stories and counterstories to give voice to African American fathers and to show the involvement that African American fathers have in their children's lives. The counterstories of African American fathers in this study challenge the master deficient narrative related to African American fathers and African American males. African American fathers play an important role in the lives of their children, families, and communities. African American fathers are dynamic partners in education.

References

Abel, Y. (2012). African American fathers' involvement in their children's school-based lives. *The Journal of Negro Education*, 81(2), 162–172.

Allen, Q. (2012). "They think minority means lesser than": Black middle-class sons and fathers resisting microaggressions in the school. *Urban Education*, 48(2), 171–197.

Bell, D.A. (1995). Who's afraid of critical race theory? *University of Illinois Law Review*, 1995 (4), 893–910.

Berry, R.Q., III, Thunder, K., & McClain, O.L. (2011). Counter narratives: Examining the mathematics and racial identities of Black boys who are successful with school mathematics. *Journal of African American Males in Education*, 2, 1.

Boyd-Franklin, N. (2003). *Black families in therapy: Understanding the African American experience* (2nd ed.). New York, NY: Guilford Press.

Bruner, J. (1990). *Acts of meaning*. Cambridge, MA: Harvard University Press.

Bruner, J. (2004). Life as narrative. *Social Research*, 71, 3.

Chase, S.E. (2005). Narrative inquiry: Multiple lenses, approaches, voices. In N.K. Denzin & Y.S. Lincoln (Eds.), *The Sage handbook of qualitative research* (3rd ed., pp. 651–679). Thousand Oaks, CA: Sage Publications, Inc.

Clandinin, D.J., & Connelly, F.M. (2000). *Narrative inquiry: Experience and story in qualitative research*. San Francisco, California: Jossey-Bass, Inc.

Coles, R.L., & Green, C. (2010). Introduction. In R.L. Coles & C. Green (Eds.), *The myth of the missing Black father* (pp. 1–16). New York, NY: Columbia University Press.

Connor, M.E. & White, J.L. (Eds.). (2011). *Black fathers: An invisible presence in America* (2nd ed.). New York, NY: Routledge.

Delgado, R. (1995). Legal storytelling: Storytelling for oppositionists and others: A plea for narrative. In Richard Delgado (Eds.), *Critical race theory: The cutting edge* (pp. 64–74). Philadelphia, PA: Temple University Press.

Dixson, A.D., & Rousseau, C.K. (2005). And we are still not saved: Critical race theory in education ten years later. *Race Ethnicity and Education*, 8(1), 7–27.

Epstein, J. (2013). Ready or not? Preparing future educators for school, family and community partnerships. *Teaching Education*, 24(2), 115–118.

Fagan, J. (2000). African American and Puerto Rican American parenting styles, paternal involvement, and head start children's social competence. *Merrill Palmer Quarterly*, 46(4), 592–612.

Foster, M. (1990). The politics of race: Through the eyes of African American teachers. *The Journal of Education*, 172(3), 123–141.

Grantham, T.C., & Henfield, M.S. (2011). Black father involvement in gifted education: Thoughts from Black fathers on increasing/improving Black father/gifted teacher partnerships. *Gifted Child Today*, 34, 4.

Hattery, A.J., & Smith, E. (2007). *African American families*. Thousand Oaks, CA: Sage.

Hutchinson, E.O. (1996). *The assassination of the Black male image*. New York, NY: Simon & Schuster.

Jeynes, W.H. (2005). The effects of parental involvement on the academic achievement of African American youth. *The Journal of Negro Education*, 74(3), 260–274.

Ladson-Billings, G. (1998). Just what is critical race theory and what's it doing in a nice field like education? *International Journal of Qualitative Studies in Education*, 11(1), 7–24.

Ladson-Billings, G., & Donnor, J. (2005). The moral activist role of critical race theory scholarship. In N.K. Denzine & Y.S. Lincoln (Eds.), *The Sage handbook of qualitative research: Third edition* (pp. 279–303). Thousand Oaks, California: Sage Publications, Inc.

Ladson-Billings, G., & Tate, W., IV (1995). Toward a critical race theory of education. *Teachers College Record*, 97, 1.

Lamb, M.E. (1987). (Ed.). *The father's role: Cross cultural perspectives*. Hillside, NJ: Lawrence Erlbaum Associates, Inc.

Lamb, M.E., Pleck, J.H., Charnov, E.L., & Levine, J.A. (1985). Paternal behavior in humans. *American Zoologist*, 25(3), 883–889.

Lareau, A. (1987). Social class and family school relationships: The importance of cultural capital. *Sociology of Education*, 56, 73–85.

McFadden, K., Tamis-LeMonda, C.S., & Cabrera, N.J. (2011). Quality matters: Low-income fathers' engagement in learning activities in early childhood predict children's academic performance in fifth grade. *Family Science*, 2(2), 120–130.

Milner IV, H.R. (2012). Challenging negative perceptions of Black teachers. *Educational Foundations*, 26, 27–46.

Reynolds, R.E., Howard, T.C., & Jones, T.K. (2013). *Is this what educators really want? Transforming the discourse on Black fathers and their participation in schools. Race, Ethnicity and Education*. doi:10.1080/13613324.2012.759931.

Solorzano, D.G., & Yasso, T.J. (2001). Critical race and Latcrit theory and method: Counterstorytelling. *International Journal of Qualitative Studies in Education*, 14(4), 471–495.

Solorzano, D.G., & Yasso, T.J. (2002). Critical race methodology: Counter storytelling as an analytical framework for education research. *Qualitative Inquiry*, 8(1), 23–24.

Tate IV, W. (1997). Critical race theory and education: History, theory, and implications. *Review of Research in Education*, 22, 195–247.

7 Engaging and Working with African American Fathers in Child Welfare

A Glimpse into the System and the Lives of Foster Fathers in Louisiana

Ruby Norris Freeman and Latrice Rollins

Introduction

I often wonder how my life and my work would have been different if both my adoptive and biological fathers had lived to raise me. I learned of my biological father when I was 19 years old, and within six months of being introduced to him, he died. My adoptive father was with me for the first 10 years of my life. It was during those 10 years of spending time with my adoptive father that I learned what it meant to have a father in the home. He was the primary provider and he treated me as if I were the only thing that mattered in the world. During a time when African Americans were in a struggle for basic American rights and human dignity, and when men were perceived to be less active in rearing children, my father adopted me.

It is imperative in understanding the child welfare system in Louisiana that a bird's eye view of the culture, lifestyle and overall character of the state is considered. Louisiana is a part of the states (Georgia, Alabama, South Carolina, Mississippi, and Louisiana) that make up the Deep South (American Heritage Dictionary, 2016). Historically, the Deep South are those states that were most dependent on plantations and slave societies during the pre-Civil War period (Roller, Twyman, Craven, & Agrantham, 1979). After the Civil War, the enslaved people were freed, with many remaining in the Deep South to work as rural workers, tenant farmers, and sharecroppers. However, beginning in the early 20th century and up to 1970, a total of six million African American people left the South to find work and other opportunities in the industrial cities of the Northeast, Midwest, and West. Thereafter, because of relative isolation and lack of economic development, the rural communities in the Deep South faced acute poverty, rural exodus, inadequate education programs, low educational attainment, poor health care, urban decay, substandard housing, and high levels of crime and unemployment (Wilkerson, 2016). Today, Louisiana is a "Red State" and is still battling the effects of the Great Migration and the remnants of Jim Crow laws (Battaglio, 2016).

The State of Louisiana has been well known for the highest number of imprisoned people in the world. The current Louisiana incarceration rate is

719 per 100,000 people and has recently been labeled, "America's Most Violent State." The violent crime rate is 557 per 100,000 residents, which is the fourth highest in the United States. The murder rate is 12.4 per 100,000 residents, which is the highest in the nation (Stebbins, 2019). Further, the number of children living in poverty has often resulted in Louisiana coming in last in the economic well-being of children. The Annie E. Casey Foundation's 2019 Kids Count Profile ranks Louisiana as 50th, compared to all states, in its number of children in poverty: 307,000 children in poverty, 371,000 children whose parents lack secure employment, 330,000 children living in households with a high housing cost burden, and 27,000 teens not in school and not working (Annie E. Casey Foundation, 2019).

Louisiana's encounters with poverty, unemployment, crime, and low educational attainment have an overwhelming effect on the state's welfare services. The social and economic condition of the state plays a significant role in the amount and kind of services that are afforded to foster care families. Louisiana certainly has its share of social and economic problems, and at times the foster care system has failed families. Studies in other states highlight that foster parents do not feel valued or trusted, experience difficulties with the fostering system, and have a preference for peer support and their own resources rather than rely on those provided by support agencies (Hendrix & Ford, 2003; Rosenwalde, 2008). Conversely, Denby and Rindfleisch (1996) found that African American foster parents' experiences with agency workers are generally favorable. Areas of improvement were noted though and focused on agency policy issues concerning reimbursement, training content, allowances for children's care, amount of services provided to parents, types of children placed with parents, and involuntary closure of homes. Warde (2008) suggests African American foster parents prioritize caring responsibilities over working with partnering agencies, which may subsequently be misunderstood by practitioners working with foster parents.

Overall, it is the caring nature of the people of our great state that has enabled our foster care system to succeed in fulfilling the mission of ensuring that Louisiana's families, children, and individuals are safe, thriving, and self-sufficient. Currently, there are more than 4,000 Louisiana children in foster care (Annie E. Casey Foundation, 2019). Individuals are encouraged to become foster parents through foster care and adoption programs offered by the state's child welfare agency. Family members, fictive kin, as well as nonrelatives may qualify as a foster parent. Financial assistance, training, and support of child welfare professionals are furnished by the state to assist foster parents in providing safe environments for foster children.

Foster fathers play an important role in foster care, but their stories are rarely shared (Gilligan, 2000; Wilson, Fyson, & Newstone, 2007). Most foster family households include a man fostering alongside a woman, so it is surprising that there is little work focusing on foster fathers (McDermid, Holmes, Kirton, & Signoretta, 2012; Orme & Combs-Orme, 2014). There are even fewer focused on African American foster fathers. Child welfare workers may underestimate the involvement of foster fathers in the care of foster children. Workers tended to view mothers as having more responsibility than fathers (Rhodes, Orme, & McSurdy, 2003). However, there is a lack of studies within this area based on the perspectives and experiences of the professionals on the frontlines (Saleh, 2013).

Foster fathers are unique because they do not share the same position as biological fathers. They are constrained from functioning in the same way as other fathers. Davids (1973) notes that foster fathers are not the highest authority in the child's life. Therefore, the state welfare system occupies the "traditional provider" role, and these fathers are required to abide by the placing agency's guidelines related to the child. These parents have a unique role that integrates family and agency responsibilities. In addition to including children from multi-problem families with emotional or health problems into their families, they work as part of the system charged with children's care. They respond to decisions about reunification and permanency planning over which they have no control. They help children deal with emotional issues of separation, attachment, and uncertainty and support children's connections with birth families. They assess children's needs, then implement programs to enhance children's development and coordinate care with medical, mental health, and educational services (Rhodes et al., 2003).

In spite of this, foster fathers are committed men with strong feelings of direct relatedness to the child and clear ideas of their fatherly responsibility. (Inch, 1999). Inch (1999) suggested foster fathers seek to promote values in children, with their desire to guide younger people and contribute to the next generation. Furthermore, Boffey (2011) affirms men can contribute positively to foster care by being good role models. Gilligan (2012) promotes the idea that foster fathers replicate gendered norms by engaging children in socially worthwhile activities that prioritize acceptable behavior. Therefore, foster fathers adopt specific roles, such as male role modeling and supporting children in activities (Gilligan, 2000, 2012; Newstone, 2000; Wilson et al., 2007). However, some studies indicate that foster fathers negotiate child-focused parenting roles that challenge and rework what it means to be a father and suggest they parent in non-normative ways to counter foster children's possible abusive experiences of fathering in birth families before foster care (Newstone, 2000; Riggs, Delfabbro, & Augoustinos, 2010).

Practice

In Louisiana, the Department of Children and Family Services is charged with the task of caring for children in foster care. Children who are in foster care were removed from their families by child protection services in order to provide them with a safe, permanent environment. In some cases, reunification with the parents or living with other relatives are the only options for a child and is in the best interest of the child. Over 400,000 children enter foster care in the United States each year (U.S. Department of Health and Human Services, 2018). African American children are disproportionately represented in the foster care system. In June of this year, the Louisiana legislature extended the age of foster care children to 21. This extension allows the Department of Children and Family Services to provide intensive services to aid in a child's transition to adulthood and to improve outcomes for foster children.

Most foster care children are in the care of the state due to abuse, neglect, or abandonment. The need to provide for these children is a tremendous burden upon society. Foster parents have the important role of teaching children what a family looks and feels like. Thorough foster parenting, children get the individual attention and guidance they need to help them develop into healthy, successful adults.

The Louisiana Department of Children and Family Services have established standards for foster parenting. To become a certified foster parent in Louisiana requires the following:

- At least 21 years of age
- Single, married, divorced, or widowed
- Financially stable (able to meet own family's needs)
- Good physical, emotional, and mental health
- Adequate space in home for additional child
- Pass state and federal criminal clearances
- Attend 21 hours of pre-service training
- Participate in home study process

In addition to the above requirements, a foster parent must attend an orientation meeting to learn more about the certification process; all adult members of the household must be fingerprinted, provide documentation from a physician that all members of the household are free of communicable disease, and provide at least five references.

There are various reasons to become a certified foster parent. Some parents have become foster parents to fulfill a calling or mission in their lives to help those in need. There are hundreds of children in the foster care system who have been abused, neglected, and abandoned and who face tremendous obstacles. Foster parenting is a wonderful way to positively impact the lives of children in a significant way. Foster parents are only one factor in the foster care system. The foster parent along with child protective services, counselors, therapists, and physicians all play an integral role in rejuvenating a broken child. Becoming a foster parent can break generational curses. The lessons taught by foster parents can change the direction of a family by instilling in a child a new sense of purpose and value that will remain with a child a lifetime. Foster parenting also provides a family atmosphere to children who have never experienced the bonds of a family or the stability of solid parental relationships and support.

Adoption creates a permanent legal relationship between a child and their adoptive family when the reunification of children with their parents is not an option. More than 60% of children in foster care spend two to five years in the system before being adopted. Almost 20% of children spend five of more years in foster care before being adopted. Some children never get adopted. In the United States, no more than 2% of Americans actually adopt children and no more than one-third have even considered adoption. The average child waits for an adoptive family for more than three years. The average age of children waiting to be adopted is 8 years old (Adoption Network, 2014). The average age of Louisiana's adopted children is 5.8 years.

Case Study

While working in the child welfare division of the Louisiana Department of Children and Family services, I had the privilege of engaging two foster fathers and would like to share their experiences.

A First-Time Foster Father

KFJ is a 32-year-old married man who is a drill instructor at an alternative school. KFJ is the oldest of seven children. He and his wife decided to become certified foster parents for several reasons. KFJ does not have biological children of his own; however, he has a stepdaughter with his wife. Whereas the couple had been married several years and had been unsuccessful in having a child of their own, the couple decided to become certified foster parents. Also, through KFJ's work as a drill instructor at an alternative school, KFJ has encountered several children who have experienced abuse and neglect or had an unstable home environment. KFJ and his wife would like to adopt a child and decided to become foster parents to give a child a positive chance at life.

KFJ learned about the foster care system through his job, where he had met several students at the school who were in foster care. Those foster care students had mixed emotions about their foster families with whom they had both good and bad experiences and felt that the system had saved their lives. He also discussed the issue with his family and discovered that an uncle had been a foster parent to several children. It was amazing to discover that some of his cousins had been foster children and had been adopted. KFJ also wanted to become a foster parent as a part of his Christian journey because he had prayed for direction and guidance in pursuing an opportunity to positively change a child's life.

KFJ became the foster father of twin toddlers, a boy and a girl, who turned two years old while in the care of KFJ and his wife. The twins came into care due to neglect. Their mother reported to child protection services because she and the twins had been living in a car and she was addicted to drugs. When the twins came into the home of KFJ, they were nonverbal, not potty trained, exhibited very low social skills, and had significant health issues.

The experience of caring for the twins greatly affected the lifestyle of KFJ in several ways. Since the twins had significant health problems, there were various doctor appointments that caused the foster parents to miss work. The weekly scheduled visitations with the mother and very little downtime became very stressful for KFJ. Also, KFJ believed the department offered little support as far as working closely with the foster parent, was not forthcoming with vital information about the background of the twins, and provided untimely notice of doctor appointments for the twins, and KFJ felt the caseworkers often times just said things to make him feel comfortable.

KFJ described his overall foster care experience as bittersweet. He was disappointed with the department's role in the process. However, when asked whether he would foster a child again, KFJ stated without hesitation that he certainly would do so. KFJ and his wife greatly impacted the lives of the twins. The foster children were noncommunicative when they came into the home of KFJ. After only six months, with the love and support of KFJ and his family, the twins learned to talk, and their social skills improved significantly. KFJ expressed the impact of his experience with the twins as life changing and as an amazing opportunity to be a part of the transformation of a person's life.

A Court Ordered Safety Monitor and Foster Father

RLH was court ordered to monitor and become the foster father of a newborn baby boy. RLH is 56 years old and is a Lieutenant with the local police department with over 30 years in law enforcement. He is a father to four children who are all adults. RLH and his wife were the fictive parents to a niece who had given birth to a drug-affected newborn. RLH was initially very skeptical about working with the department and about raising a baby who would require a lot of time and attention. However, after recognizing the innocence of the child and wanting the child to have a good chance at life, RLH decided to accept the challenge of foster parenting.

A court-ordered safety plan is implemented by the court when there is a unit of family support available to a parent who is involved in an investigation by the department and removal is not in the best interest of the child. A safety monitor is a family member or family friend who is appointed by the court to assist the parent in the care of the child in accordance with the instructions of the court. The safety monitor also informs the court and the department of any inconsistent behavior of the parent that is harmful to the child.

RLH as a safety monitor was required to become a certified foster parent. He and his wife completed the 21-hour pre-service training and all of the other requirements. RLH found the certification process beneficial and relevant in describing the many issues that face foster parents. The courses also provided helpful recommendations to resolve critical issues.

Becoming a safety monitor and foster father positively affected RLH's family and friends. RLH's children have become attached to the foster child, and they also assist with providing care and support for the foster child. RLH's church community has welcomed the foster child as a part of the church family and has helped and encouraged the family. Through the church, RLH discovered other church members who were also foster parents. RLH describes his experience as a foster father as rewarding and satisfying to his soul. RLH cherishes the opportunity to personally observe the foster child's development and progress. RLH states that he has spent more time with his foster child than with his own children as they were growing up. He thinks of his foster child as a son and has a strong relationship with the child. RLH is a hands-on foster parent and helps with the day-to-day routine activities such as taking the child to doctor appointments, getting haircuts, bathing, and teaching life lessons. RLH takes a lot of pride in providing a well-rounded, secure, and happy home environment for the child that allows the child to be a fun-loving kid.

RLH describes his overall foster care experience as rewarding, and his contact with the department as fair. RLH enjoys watching his foster child grow and thrive and especially seeing the child overcome obstacles. RLH's relationship with the department has been somber in that RLH recognizes the difficult and overwhelming conditions facing the department. RLH works in law enforcement, so he understands the pressure facing the department as it navigates working with many unstable families. Difficulties RLH has faced in foster parenting involve establishing a healthy relationship with the biological parents, navigating the court system, adjusting to new caseworkers, and sometimes receiving inaccurate and inconsistent information from the department. When asked whether he would foster other children, RLH replied that if there is a need, he would like to be of service.

Lessons Learned

Foster care, as a protective service, is a temporary means of safeguarding children until unsafe conditions in their home have been mitigated. The primary goal of foster care is reunifying children with their biological families. In addition to providing a safe environment for children, foster parents are to assist in reconnecting a foster child with his or her family. Many times, foster parents are interested in foster care programs as a means to conveniently adopt children. Reunification efforts by foster parents are sometimes misplaced when foster children are in foster homes. Foster parents become emotionally attached to foster children and on occasion advocate against the child welfare agency in the reunification of foster children with their biological parents.

The ability of foster parents to render care to foster children greatly depends upon the transparency of the child welfare agency. It is imperative that the child welfare agency is open, honest, and straightforward about the physical, and emotional conditions and needs of foster children. Most foster parents, including fathers, are committed to providing stable, loving, and safe environments for foster children. However, the capacity of foster parents to assist foster children is dependent upon being properly informed of any critical factor affecting the well-being of foster children. The child welfare agency is obligated to provide for the best interest of foster children and should properly communicate timely, pertinent information regarding the care of foster children while emphasizing the role of foster parents in the reunification of foster children with their families.

Conclusion

Louisiana's child welfare system has its share of discrepancies as do all other agencies tasked with the responsibility of safeguarding families, children, and individuals. However, during the last year, the Louisiana Department of Children and Family Services reached a milestone by setting a record for finalized adoptions with 912 children finding loving, permanent homes with 631 families. Also, 2,332 children were reunified with their families, either returning home or to the custody or guardianship of a relative (Louisiana Department of Children & Family Services, 2019). In addition to the work done by the department, the Louisiana Foster & Adoptive Parent Association is a parent group that provides support and resources to foster, adoptive, and kinship families about resources available in their communities. Its mission is to empower foster and adoptive parents and children in their care by providing communication, support, training, and advocacy services.

As an attorney in child welfare, my primary duty is the representation of the department in safeguarding families. Also, when parents cannot responsibly care for their children, I represent the department in involuntarily terminating the parental rights of parents and certifying the freedom of children for adoption. My work is challenging and most times staggering, yet the reward of transforming the lives of children is immensely satisfying.

Those foster parents who foster children and most times adopt them save the lives of broken children. A few studies highlight the varied and diverse ways men care for children as foster fathers and indicate how their engagement by the foster care system could be improved (Davids, 1973; Heslop, 2019). The cases shared here indicate that foster fathers need to be acknowledged more for their role in, and contribution to, the development of children. These foster fathers concluded that foster parents can positively transform the lives of foster children, and the transformation of foster children can last a lifetime. I agree. I am a product of the love, support, and sacrifice of my adoptive father, John "Papa" Norris, whose name I proudly display daily: Ruby Norris Freeman.

References

American Heritage® *dictionary of the English language.* (2016). (5th ed.). Houghton Mifflin Harcourt Publishing Company.

Adoption Network. (2014). *US adoption statistics.* Retrieved from https://adoptionnetwork.com/adoption-statistics.

Annie E. Casey Foundation. (2019). *2019 kids count profile.* Retrieved from https://www.aecf.org/m/databook/2019KC_profile_LA.pdf.

Battaglio, S. (November 3, 2016). When red meant Democratic and blue was Republican. A brief history of TV electoral maps. *Los Angeles Times.* Retrieved from November 28, 2018.

Boffey, M. (2011). *Men are good foster carers, too.* London, UK: The Fostering Network.

Davids, L. (1973). Foster fatherhood: The untapped resource. *Child Welfare,* 52(2), 100–108.

Denby, R., & Rindfleisch, N. (1996). African Americans' foster parenting experiences: Research findings and implications for policy and practice. *Children and Youth Services Review,* 18(6), 523–551.

Gilligan, R. (2000). Men as foster carers: A neglected resource. *Adoption and Fostering,* 24(2), 63–69. doi:10.1177/030857590002400209.

Gilligan, R. (2012). Promoting a sense of "secure base" for children in foster care—Exploring the potential contribution of foster fathers. *Journal of Social Work Practice: Psychotherapeutic Approaches in Health, Welfare and the Community,* 26(4), 473–486. doi:10.1080/02650533.2012.709229.

Hendrix, S., & Ford, J. (2003). Hardiness of foster families and the intent to continue to foster. *Journal of Family Social Work,* 7(2), 25–34. doi:10.1300/J039v07n02_03.

Heslop, P. (2019). Foster fathers performing gender: The negotiation and reproduction of parenting roles in families who foster. *Journal of Family Social Work,* 22(4-5), 352–368.

Inch, L.J. (1999). Aspects of foster parenting. *Child & Adolescent Social Work Journal,* 16(5), 393–412. doi:0.1023/A:1022399813438.

Louisiana Department of Children & Family Services. (2019). *Foster parenting.* Retrieved from http://dcfs.la.gov/page/374.

McDermid, S., Holmes, L., Kirton, D., & Signoretta, P. (2012). *The demographic characteristics of foster carers in the UK: Motivations, barriers and messages for recruitment and retention.* Loughborough, London, Canterbury: The Childhood Wellbeing Research Centre.

Newstone, S. (2000). Male foster carers: What do we mean by "role models". *Adoption & Fostering,* 24(3), 36–47. doi: 10.1177/030857590002400306.

Orme, J., & Combs-Orme, T. (2014). Foster parenting together: Foster parent couples. *Children and Youth Services Review,* 36, 124–132. doi:10.1016/j.childyouth.2013.11.017.

Rhodes, K.W., Orme, J.G., & McSurdy, M. (2003). Foster parent's role performance responsibilities: Perceptions of foster mothers, fathers, and workers. *Children and Youth Services Review,* 25(12), 935–964.

Riggs, W., Delfabbro, P., & Augoustinos, M. (2010). Foster fathers and carework: Engaging alternative models of parenting. *Fathering,* 8(1), 24–36. doi:10.3149/fth.0801.24.

Roller, D.C., Twyman, R.W., Craven, A.O., & Agrantham, D.W. (1979). *The encyclopedia of Southern history.* Louisiana State University Press.

Rosenwalde, M. (2008). Foster parents speak: Preferred characteristics of foster children and experiences in the role of foster parent. *Journal of Family Social Work,* 11(3), 287–302. doi:10.1080/10522150802292376.

Saleh, M.F. (2013). Child welfare professionals' experiences in engaging fathers in services. *Child and Adolescent Social Work Journal*, 30(2), 119–137.

Stebbins, S. (July 16, 2019). America's most violent state? Louisiana. What's the most peaceful one? *USA Today*. Retrieved from August 1, 2019.

US Department of Health and Human Services, Administration for Children and Families, Administration on Children, Youth, and Families, Children's Bureau. (2018). *Adoption foster care analysis reporting system (AFCARS), FY 2009–2018*. Retrieved from https://www.acf.hhs.gov/cb/resource/trends-in-foster-care-and-adoption.

Warde, B. (2008). Role perceptions of foster care in African American kinship and nonkinship foster parents: A quantitative analysis. *Journal of Family Social Work*, 11(3), 272–286. doi: 10.1080/0522150802292228.

Wilkerson, I. (2016). The long-lasting legacy of the Great Migration. *Smithsonian Magazine*, 9. Retrieved from https://www.smithsonianmag.com/history/long-lasting-legacy-great-migration-180960118/.

Wilson, K., Fyson, R., & Newstone, S. (2007). Foster fathers: Their experiences and contributions to fostering. *Child & Family Social Work*, 12(1), 22–31. doi:10.1111/j.1365-2206.2006.00443.x.

8 Engaging and Working with African American Fathers in Mental Health Services

Latrice Rollins and Kisha Thomas

Introduction

Depression has been described as an epidemic in the United States, with lifetime incidence rates estimated at 17% in women and 9% in men (American Psychiatric Association, 2013; Centers for Disease Control and Prevention CDC, 2010; Grigoriadis & Robinson, 2007; Rosenthal, Learned, Liu, & Weitzman, 2013; Wainwright & Surtees, 2002). Singleton, Bumpstead, O'Brien, Lee, and Meltzer (2001) indicated that the gender gap in depression may be smaller than previously estimated. Further, research suggests that depression is an important problem for large numbers of African American men in the United States. However, depression among African American men, especially among African American fathers, remains relatively understudied (Gary, 1985; Watkins, Green, Rivers, & Rowell, 2006). Limited empirical evidence exists regarding national prevalence rates of mental illness, the correlates of such illness, and service use among fathers (Nicholson, Nason, Calabresi, & Yando, 1999). Sinkewicz and Lee (2011) found that the prevalence of 12-month major depressive episode (12%) is one and a half times higher among African American fathers than among men in the general population. Further, clinical issues affecting African American males' depression rates may be related to limited access to care and lower rates of men seeking mental health services (Addis & Mahalik, 2003; D'Augelli & Vallance, 1981; Padesky & Hammen, 1981; Vessey & Howard, 1993). As a result of the lower rates of access and help seeking by men, it may appear that they experience bias in diagnoses.

African American men are disproportionately exposed to adverse social and economic factors that may be linked to depression (Sinkewicz & Lee, 2011). African American men often face more psychosocial stressors, such as racism and discrimination, than other racial/ethnic groups (Hamer, 1997; Johnson, 1998; Mizell, 1999; Roy, 1999). Dunkel Schetter et al. (2013) reported higher rates of racism reported by African American fathers in comparison to Latino fathers. Past research has demonstrated the adverse effects of racism on mental health outcomes reported by African American populations (Jackson et al., 1996; Schmitt, Branscombe, Postmes, & Garcia, 2014; Williams & Mohammed, 2009).

Specifically, with men, these effects have been attributed in part to feelings of helplessness, hopelessness, and invisibility that accompany being a target of racism (Bamishigbin et al., 2017; Clark, Anderson, Clark, & Williams, 1999).

Life or family stress and low social support are risk factors associated with depression among fathers (Spector, 2006). Poverty, physical health problems, having a child with special health care needs, maternal depressive symptoms, and unemployment have been independently associated with paternal depressive symptoms, with unemployment associated with the highest rates of such problems (Rosenthal et al., 2013). Experiencing stressful life events such as health, work, family, personal and social matters, and financial concerns increases the odds that African American males will suffer from a major depression (Brown, Ahmed, Gary, & Milburn, 1995). The increased risk of mental illness on the basis of socioeconomic variables is consistent with previous findings for urban African American fathers with depression (Sinkewicz & Lee, 2011). Depression has also been shown to decrease the economic well-being of men and their families (Danziger, Corcoran, & Danziger, 2003). Knowledge of the mental health conditions among African American fathers may improve the efficacy of labor market interventions for these men, which have thus far been less successful than those for women (Sinkewicz & Lee, 2011).

Bowman's (1990) seminal work on African American fathers found that role strain or perceived stress that emerges as a result of social responsibilities (e.g., fathering) was negatively related to African American fathers' satisfaction with their family lives. Cabrera and Mitchell (2009) found that fathers who reported higher levels of parenting stress were *more* frequently engaged in management or caregiving activities, such as waking up at night with their child. Correctly understood, African American fathers can be fully understood only in relation to the interaction of their psychological health, culture, family relationships, and social class (Coll et al., 1996; McAdoo, 1993; Watkins 2010; Spencer, Dupree, & Hartmann, 1997).

Unmarried fathers hold significant interest because there is reason to hypothesize that their mental health status is systematically different from married fathers (Sinkewicz, 2006). They are also the fastest growing contingent of fathers, the group of fathers about which the least is known, and a population of men often targeted negatively by public policy (Sinkewicz & Lee, 2011). Fathers' never-married status did not, surprisingly, increase the risk of any lifetime or 12-month mental disorder. Additionally, studies focused on divorced fathers found that post-divorce visits with children "can lead to depression and sorrow in men who love their children" and many divorced fathers are "overwhelmed by feelings of failure and self-hatred," and as a result are "disengaging from a family that is no longer really theirs" (Bartlett, 2004, p. 165). African American fathers who were divorced, separated, or widowed were more than twice as likely as married or cohabitating fathers to be at risk for any 12-month and lifetime disorders.

Fatherhood status may either increase or decrease risk for mental illness among men (Garfield, Clark-Kauffman, & Davis, 2006). The provision of mental health services specifically designed to meet the needs of fathers may pay large dividends in improved family relationships. Parent–child relationships are deemed important not only to child development but also to the healthy functioning of African American men. (Baker, 2014). In addition, the possibility that father–child contact may prove to be a protective factor for the mental health of fathers deserves consideration. Although fathers' involvement with their children, including their monetary contribution and emotional support, are acknowledged, little has been done to identify the factors related to fathers' emotional and psychological well-being, which, in turn, may influence their ability to parent (Fagan, 1996; Jackson, 1999; Kelley, Smith, Green, Berndt, & Rogers, 1998; Moore, 1998). Studies that have investigated the relationship between parent-reported depression and parenting practices have focused predominantly on mothers. Depression can manifest as physical or emotional distress and may result in marked behavioral impairment and diminished quality of parenting (Kelly & Bartley, 2010; Mensah & Kiernan, 2011; Rosenthal et al., 2013). Poor mental health decreases the quality of intimate partner and parent–child relationships (Kessler, Walter, & Forthofer, 1998; Zlotnick, Kohn, Keitner, & Grotta, 2000). Furthermore, it has adverse effects on child health and development (Downey & Coyne, 1990; Phares, 1996; Rutter & Quinton, 1984). Fathers who reported experiencing more depressive symptoms were four times more likely to engage in negative parenting (i.e., spanking) and less than half as likely to report engaging in home literacy practices (i.e., father–child reading) than fathers who experienced fewer depressive symptoms. Paulson, Keefe, and Leiferman (2009) examined psychological determinants of father involvement in a large sample of African American, White, and Hispanic fathers. They found that fathers who experienced more depressive symptoms (e.g., sadness) were less likely to engage in developmentally important parenting practices, such as father–child reading.

Male depressive symptomatology is often underestimated, undiagnosed, and untreated (Royal College of Psychiatrists, 1998). Anxiety, substance dependence, and bad health are disproportionately concentrated in African American fathers with depression (Sinkewicz & Lee, 2011). As with women, fathers will present with a dysphoric mood, but unlike their female counterparts, depressed men often experience a change in social behavior. Withdrawal from social situations, indecisiveness, cynicism, and an irritable mood are often found as hallmark signs of depression in the adult male. Depression is typically defined as parent-reported feelings of sadness, fatigue, and emotional withdrawal rather than the presence of clinically diagnosed depression (Davis, Davis, Freed, & Clark, 2011).

African American men remain one of the most underserved populations in the mental health field (Holden, McGregor, Blanks, & Mahaffey, 2012). Research has repeatedly proved that men who seek treatment, benefit from it – but they seek it out far less often than women (Cochran & Rabinowitz, 2003; Spector, 2006). Mental health services have been routinely under-utilized. Parents perceived fewer barriers and had more positive attitudes toward seeking services for their children than for themselves. Fathers and ethnic minorities utilize services the least (Thurston & Phares, 2008). Mental health service use is particularly low for African American fathers. Addressing African American fathers' mental health needs not only has potential impact for the improved psychiatric health of fathers but also for their children and families (Doyle, Joe, & Caldwell, 2012).

Practice

Max Empowerment, LLC is a private practice that provides individual counseling, group therapy, and couples and family counseling services. The counselors provide a supportive counseling environment for children, teens, adults, and couples. They are committed to helping their clients reach their personal and professional goals through counseling. Through a collaborative counseling approach, goals are established to assist clients with self-actualization. They also provide support to other counseling professionals through super-vision, consultation, and training services.

Typically, a referral for counseling services comes from a Google search or a referral from a health care provider. Clients may also reach out to their insurance providers to find resources for mental health services. Fathers do not typically come in as much with their children for services. However, there are quite a few male clients who seek services for themselves. These clients are typically ready to change and consistent in treatment when they are reaching out on their own. They realize that they need to do something different because their behavior is affecting their family, their children, or their job. The court ordered or mandated clients are typically not as compliant or open to change.

Case Study

The client is a 35-year-old African American married father of three. He was dealing with anger management issues and how to appropriately dis-cipline his child. We discovered that there was some underlying trauma that was never resolved that was still affecting him. He was open with sharing, so we were able to work through that. We were able to have him identify the norm and understand his relationship with his parents were not the typical parent–child relationship; it was an abusive situation. Resolving his past trauma helped to shed some light on how he was interacting with his own family. He was mimicking some of the same negative behaviors that he experienced when he was being raised. After working through it, we acknowledged that his unresolved trauma caused his depression. Depression can manifest itself in many different ways, such as isolation or anger. It can go from one extreme to another. He initially came for anger management that affected the family, work, and relationships with other people. His behavior was not just isolated to one domain.

Strategies

Recognizing the negative psychological consequences of depression and the ensuing barriers to "responsible" fathering seems to be a necessary first step (Brewer, 1998; Hoard & Anderson, 2004). Screening fathers for depression must be increased in health care and social service settings. Furthermore, providers should consider how African American fathers' social, economic, and familial experiences may impact their mental health (Doyle et al., 2012). Many treatments have proven effective for depressed fathers including traditional psychodynamic, cognitive behavioral therapy, and group therapy. However, there is a need for culturally relevant, male-specific tools or programs to prevent and treat depression among African American fathers (Sinkewicz & Lee, 2011). Interventions that target race-related stressors and provide culturally appropriate coping strategies may promote better outcomes in this important and understudied population. More active forms of coping such as problem solving and seeking support are probably better alternatives for fathers (Bamishigbin et al., 2017). These programs should also focus on the various stages of help seeking, including recognizing the problem, deciding to seek help, and selecting where to get services (Cauce et al., 2002; Thurston & Phares, 2008). Couples therapy is effective because it allows the fathers' partner to help identify behaviors and depressive symptoms that the father is not conscious of and sometimes before the depression actually happens. The partner can notice the changes before the client may see it.

Therapy is effective when it can be initiated and continued, but research repeatedly shows that men seek it out far less than women. Effective outreach programs to encourage treatment among depressed fathers are recommended (Spector, 2006). Providers may need to be more flexible with mode of delivery of treatment, developing strategies to decrease premature dropout from treatment, matching interventions to families' needs, and being culturally sensitive to clients (Phelps, Brown, & Power, 2002; Snell-Johns, Mendez, & Smith, 2004; Thurston & Phares, 2008). Phares, Fields, and Binitie (2006) described several strategies that can be used to engage fathers in treatment, including increasing family-related training in graduate programs, inviting fathers to participate in treatment and intervening when they are hesitant, and creating a father-friendly environment (Thurston & Phares, 2008).

Lessons Learned

African American fathers are willing to get mental health services and treatment when they are ready to get help. Therefore, it is really important to meet them where they are and try to implement best practices. Additionally, when working with African American fathers, there are a lot of layers, and once they begin to share, all kind of needs arise, even though they may have presented for only one thing. This is a result of men not having a safe space to really talk and share. Therefore, once they get help, issues that they have not dealt with arise because they have not had the opportunity for anybody to listen or to share it with anybody. This case also highlights the need for providers to acknowledge African American fathers' adverse childhood experiences and trauma exposure in their homes, communities, and society (Bocknek, Lewis, & Raveau, 2017). Providers should embrace strategies that are trauma informed and healing centered (Evans, Hemmings, Burkhalter, & Lacy, 2016; Ginwright, 2018; Rich 2016).

References

Addis, M.E., & Mahalik, J.R. (2003). Men, masculinity, and the contexts of help seeking. *American Psychologist*, 58(1), 5–14.

American Psychiatric Association. (2013). *Diagnostic and statistical manual of mental disorders (DSM-5®)*. American Psychiatric Pub.

Baker, C.E. (2014). African American fathers' depression and stress as predictors of father involvement during early childhood. *Journal of African American Psychology*, 40(4), 311–333.

Bamishigbin, O.N., Dunkel Schetter, C., Guardino, C.M., Stanton, A.L., Schafer, P., Shalowitz, M., & Raju, T. (2017). Risk, resilience, and depressive symptoms in low-income African American fathers. *Cultural Diversity and Ethnic Minority Psychology*, 23(1), 70.

Bartlett, E.E. (2004). The effects of fatherhood on the health of men: a review of the literature. *Journal of Men's Health and Gender*, 1(2-3), 159–169.

Bocknek, E.L., Lewis, M.L., & Raveau, H.A. (2017). *African American fathers' mental health & child well-being: A cultural practices, strengths-based perspective*. I. Iruka, S. Curenton, & T. Durden (Eds.), *African American children in early childhood education: Making the case for policy investments in families, schools, and communities*, (pp. 221–243).

Bowman, P.J. (1990). Coping with provider role strain: Adaptive cultural resources among African American husband-fathers. *Journal of African American Psychology*, 16, 1–21.

Brewer, A.M. (1998). The relationships among gender role conflict, depression, hopelessness, and marital satisfaction in a sample of African American men. *Dissertation Abstracts International: Section B: The Sciences and Engineering*, 59(6), 3049.

Brown, D.R., Ahmed, F., Gary, L.E., & Milburn, N.G. (1995). Major depression in a community sample of African Americans. *American Journal of Psychiatry*, 152(3), 373–378.

Cabrera, N.J., & Mitchell, S.J. (2009). An exploratory study of fathers parenting stress and toddlers' social development in low-income African American families. *Fathering: A Journal of Theory, Research, & Practice about Men as Fathers*, 7, 201–225.

Cauce, A.M., Domenech-Rodriguez, M., Paradise, M., Cochran, B.N., Shea, J., Srebnik, D., & Baydar, N. (2002). Cultural and contextual influences in mental health help seeking: A focus on ethnic minority youth. *Journal of Consulting and Clinical Psychology*, 70, 44–55.

Centers for Disease Control and Prevention (CDC). (2010). Current depression among adults—United States, 2006 and 2008. *Morbidity and mortality weekly report*, 59(38), 1229–1235.

Chesney, M.A., Chambers, D.B., Taylor, J.M., Johnson, L.M., & Folkman, S. (2003). Coping effectiveness training for men living with HIV: Results from a randomized clinical trial testing a group-based intervention. *Psychosomatic Medicine*, 65, 1038–1046. http://dx.doi.org/10.1097/01.PSY.0000097344.78697.ED.

Cicchetti, D., & Toth, S.L. (1998). The development of depression in children and adolescents. *American Psychologist*, 53(2), 221–241.

Clark, R., Anderson, N.B., Clark, V.R., & Williams, D.R. (1999). Racism as a stressor for African Americans. A biopsychosocial model. *American Psychologist*, 54, 805–816. http://dx.doi.org/10.1037/0003-066X.54.10.805.

Cochran, S.V., & Rabinowitz, F.E. (2003). Gender-sensitive recommendations for assessment and treatment of depression in men. *Professional Psychology: Research & Practice*, 34(2), 132–140.

Coll, C.G., Lamberty, G., Jenkins, R., McAdoo, H.P., Crnic, K., Wasik, B.H., & Garcia, H.V. (1996). An integrative model for the study of developmental competencies in minority children. *Child Development*, 67, 1891–1914.

D'Augelli, A.R., & Vallance, T.R. (1981). The helping community: Promoting mental health in rural areas through informal helping. *Journal of Rural Community Psychology*, 2(1), 3–16.

Danziger, S., Corcoran, J., & Danziger, S. (2003). Barriers to the employment of welfare recipients. In R. Cherry & W. Rodgers (Eds.), *Prosperity for all? The economic boom and African Americans* (pp. 245–278). New York, NY: Russell Sage Foundation.

Davis, R.N., Davis, M.M., Freed, G.L., & Clark, S.J. (2011). Fathers' depression related to positive and negative parenting behaviors with 1-year-old children. *Pediatrics*, 127, 612–618.

Downey, G., & Coyne, J. (1990). Children of depressed parents: An integrative review. *Psychological Review*, 108, 50–76.

Doyle, O., Joe, S., & Caldwell, C.H. (2012). Ethnic differences in mental illness and mental health service use among African American fathers. *American journal of public health*, 102(S2), S222–S231.

Dunkel Schetter, C., Schafer, P., Lanzi, R.G., Clark-Kauffman, E., Raju, T.N.K., & Hillemeier, M.M., the Community Child Health Network. (2013). Shedding light on the mechanisms underlying health disparities through community participatory methods: The stress pathway. *Perspectives on Psychological Science*, 8, 613–633. http://dx.doi.org/10.1177/1745691613506016.

Eaton, W., & Kessler, L. (1981). Rates of symptoms of depression in a national sample. *American Journal of Epidemiology*, 114, 528–538.

Evans, A.M., Hemmings, C., Burkhalter, C., & Lacy, V. (2016). Responding to race related trauma: Counseling and research recommendations to promote post-traumatic growth when counseling African American males. *The Journal of Counselor Preparation and Supervision*, 8, 1. http://dx.doi.org/ 10.7729/81.1085.

Hamer, J.F. (1997). The fathers of "fatherless" African American children. *Families in Society: The Journal of Contemporary Human Services*, 78, 564–578.

Fagan, J. (1996). A preliminary study of low-income African American fathers' play interactions with their preschool-age children. *Journal of African American Psychology*, 22(1), 7–20.

Fagan, J., Bernd, E., & Whiteman, V. (2007). Adolescent fathers' parenting stress, social support, and involvement with infants. *Journal of Research on Adolescence*, 17(1), 1–22.

Garfield, C.F., Clark-Kauffman, E., & Davis, MM (2006). Fatherhood as a component of men's health. *JAMA*, 296(19), 2365–2368.

Gary, L.E. (1985). Correlates of depressive symptoms among a select population of African American men. *American Journal of Public Health*, 75(1), 1220–1222.

Ginwright, S. (2018). *The future of healing: Shifting from trauma informed care to healing centered engagement. Occasional Paper*, 25.

Grigoriadis, S., & Robinson, G. (2007). Gender issues in depression. *Annals of Clinical Psychiatry*, 19(4), 247–255.

Hoard, L.R., & Anderson, E.A. (2004). Factors related to depression in rural and urban noncustodial, low-income fathers. *Journal of Community Psychology*, 32(1), 103–119.

Holden, K.B., McGregor, B.S., Blanks, S.H., & Mahaffey, C. (2012). Psychosocial, sociocultural, and environmental influences on mental health help-seeking among African American men. *Journal of Men's Health*, 9(2), 63–69. 10.1016/j.jomh.2012.03.002.

Jackson, A.P. (1999). The effects of nonresident father involvement on single African American mothers and their young children. *Social Work*, 44(2), 156–166.

Jackson, J.S., Brown, T.N., Williams, D.R., Torres, M., Sellers, S.L., & Brown, K. (1996). Racism and the physical and mental health status of African Americans: A thirteen year national panel study. *Ethnicity & Disease*, 6, 132–147.

Johnson, W.E. (1998). Paternal involvement in fragile, African American families: Implications for clinical social work practice. *Smith College Studies in Social Work*, 68(2), 215–231.

Kelley, M.L., Smith, T.S., Green, A.P., Berndt, A.E., & Rogers, M.C. (1998). Importance of fathers' parenting to African American toddlers' social and cognitive development. *Infant Behavior & Development*, 21(4), 733–744.

Kelly, Y., & Bartley, M. (2010). Parental and child health. In K. Hansen, H. Joshi & S. Dex (Eds.), *Children of the 21st century: The first five years* (pp. 249–264). The Policy Press.

Kessler, R., Walter, E., & Forthofer, M. (1998). The social consequences of psychiatric disorders: Probability of marital stability. *American Journal of Psychiatry*, 155, 1092–1096.

McAdoo, J. (1993). The role of African American fathers: An ecological perspective. *Families in Society: The Journal of Contemporary Human Services*, 74(1), 28–35.

McMillan, S.C., Small, B.J., Weitzner, M., Schonwetter, R., Tittle, M., Moody, L., & Haley, W.E. (2006). Impact of coping skills intervention with family caregivers of hospice patients with cancer. *Cancer*, 106, 214–222. http://dx.doi.org/10.1002/cncr.21567.

Mensah, F.K., & Kiernan, K.E. (2011). Maternal general health and children's cognitive development and behaviour in the early years: findings from the Millennium Cohort Study. *Child Care, Health and Development*, 37(1), 44–54.

Meyer, J. (2003). Improving men's health: Developing a long-term strategy. *American Journal of Public Health*, 93, 709–711.

Mizell, C.A. (1999). Life course influences on African American men's depression: Adolescent parental composition, self-concept, and adult earnings. *Journal of African American Studies*, 29(4), 467–490.

Moore, M. (1998). Children of young disadvantaged women are unlikely to receive consistent support from their fathers. *Family Planning Perspectives*, 30(6), 291–292.

Neff, J.A., & Husaini, B.A. (1980). Race, socio-economic status, and psychiatric impairment: A research note. *Journal of Community Psychology*, 8, 16–19.

Nicholson, J., Nason, M.W., Calabresi, A.O., & Yando, R. (1999). Fathers with severe mental illness: characteristics and comparisons. *American Journal of Orthopsychiatry*, 69(1), 134–141.

Padesky, C.C., & Hammen, C.L. (1981). Sex differences in depressive symptom expression and help-seeking among college students. *Sex Roles*, 7, 309–320.

Paulson, J.F., Keefe, H.A., & Leiferman, J.A. (2009). Early parental depression and child language development. *Journal of Child Psychology and Psychiatry*, 50, 254–262.

Phares, V. (1996). *Fathers and developmental psycholopathology*. New York, NY: John Wiley.

Phares, V., Fields, S., & Binitie, I. (2006). Getting fathers involved in child-related therapy. *Cognitive and Behavioral Practice*, 13, 42–52.

Phelps, L., Brown, R.T., & Power, T.J. (2002). *Pediatric psychopharmacology: Combining medical and psychosocial interventions*. Washington, DC: American Psychological Association.

Rich, J. (2016). *Moving toward healing: Trauma and violence and boys and young men of color*. Drexel University School of Public Health.

Rosenthal, D.G., Learned, N., Liu, Y.H., & Weitzman, M. (2013). Characteristics of fathers with depressive symptoms. *Maternal and Child Health Journal*, 17(1), 119–128.

Ross, J.M. (1992). *The male paradox*. New York: Simon and Schuster.

Roy, K. (1999). Low-income single fathers in an African American community and the requirements of welfare reform. *Journal of Family Issues*, 20(4), 432–457.

Royal College of Psychiatrists. (1998). *Men behaving sadly*. Royal College of Psychiatrists. www.rcpsych.ac.uk.

Rutter, M., & Quinton, D. (1984). Parental psychiatric disorder: Effects on children. *Psychological Medicine*, 14, 853–880.

Schmitt, M.T., Branscombe, N.R., Postmes, T., & Garcia, A. (2014). The consequences of perceived discrimination for psychological well-being: A meta-analytic review. *Psychological Bulletin*, 140, 921–948. http://dx.doi.org/10.1037/a0035754.

Singleton, N., Bumpstead, R., O'Brien, M., Lee, A., & Meltzer, H. (2001). *Psychiatric morbidity among adults living in private households*. London: TSO.

Sinkewicz, M. (2006). *The mental health of men: Profile and life trajectories of urban American fathers (doctoral dissertation)*. NY, USA: Columbia University.

Sinkewicz, M., & Lee, R. (2011). Prevalence, comorbidity, and course of depression among African American fathers in the United States. *Research on Social Work Practice*, 21(3), 289–297.

Snell-Johns, J., Mendez, J.L., & Smith, B.H. (2004). Evidence-based solutions for overcoming access barriers, decreasing attrition, and promoting change with underserved families. *Journal of Family Psychology*, 18, 19–35.

Spector, A.Z. (2006). Fatherhood and depression: A review of risks, effects, and clinical application. *Issues in Mental Health Nursing*, 27(8), 867–883.

Spencer, M.B., Dupree, D., & Hartmann, T. (1997). A phenomenological variant of ecological systems theory (PVEST): A self-organization perspective in context. *Development and Psychopathology*, 9, 817–833.

Thurston, I.B., & Phares, V. (2008). Mental health service utilization among African American and Caucasian mothers and fathers. *Journal of Consulting and Clinical Psychology*, 76(6), 1058.

Vessey, J.T., & Howard, K.I. (1993). Who seeks psychotherapy? *Psychotherapy*, 30, 546–553.

Wainwright, N.W.J., & Surtees, P.G. (2002). Childhood adversity, gender and depression over the life-course. *Journal of Affective Disorders*, 72(1), 33–44.

Wallerstein, J.S., & Blakeslee, S. (1989). *Second chances: Men, women, and children a decade after divorce*. New York: Ticknor and Fields.

Watkins, D.C., Green, B.L., Rivers, B.M., & Rowell, K.L. (2006). Depression in African American men: Implications for future research. *Journal of Men's Health and Gender, 3,* 227–235.

Watkins, D.C., Walker, R.L., & Griffith, D.M. (2010). A meta-study of African American male mental health and well-being. *Journal of African American Psychology, 36,* 303–330.

Williams, D.R., & Mohammed, S.A. (2009). Discrimination and racial disparities in health: Evidence and needed research. *Journal of Behavioral Medicine, 32,* 20–47. http://dx.doi.org/10.1007/s10865-008-9185-0.

Williams, T.T., Mance, G., Caldwell, C.H., & Antonucci, T.C. (2012). The role of prenatal stress and maternal emotional support on the postpartum depressive symptoms of African American adolescent fathers. *Journal of African American Psychology, 38,* 455–470.

Yancey, W., Rigsby, L., & McCarthy, J. (1972). Social position and self-evaluation: The relative importance of race. *American Journal of Sociology, 78,* 338–359.

Zlotnick, C., Kohn, R., Keitner, G., & Grotta, D. (2000). The relationship between quality of interpersonal relationships and major depressive disorder: Findings from the National Comorbidity Survey. *Journal of Affective Disorders,* 59(3), 205–215.

9 Engaging and Working with African American Fathers in Battering Intervention Programs

Latrice Rollins and Carmen Ray

Introduction

Intimate partner violence (IPV) is a significant public health problem affecting women, men, and children across the United States (Voith, Logan-Greene, Strodthoff, & Bender, 2018). IPV is defined as physical violence, sexual violence, stalking, and/or psychological aggression carried out by an individual's current or former intimate partner. (National Center for Injury Prevention and Control, 2017b). IPV can be used to control, coerce, degrade, and manipulate. Partners can employ various methods such as physical abuse, criticizing and degrading, restricting financial access, and many others as a way to deal with their frustration while controlling their family members. Fathers' use of violence can involve incidents intended to hurt the mother of their children with the fathers' full knowledge that their abuse can have a negative impact, while in other cases, the fathers may not realize their behavior can negatively affect their loved ones (Martin, 2018; Scott & Crooks, 2007; Pennell, Rikard, & Sanders-Rice, 2013).

IPV has lasting adverse consequences for survivors and their children, including poor physical health, psychological distress, and social consequences like isolation from social networks (National Center for Injury Prevention and Control, 2017a). Given the well-established, potentially devastating consequences of IPV for the entire family, there is a critical need for researchers, practitioners, and decision makers to better understand the services that exist to help prevent IPV and address it effectively when it occurs (Bair-Merritt, Blackstone, & Feudtner, 2006; Kitzmann, Gaylord, Holt, & Kenny, 2003; Wathen & MacMillan, 2013; Appel & Holden, 1998; Holden, 2003).

Continued discussions and recognition of the intersection of structural oppression, racial discrimination, poverty, housing, and IPV may play an important role in understanding how to provide meaningful support for fathers to create healthy relationships (OPRE, 2020). Additionally, the prevalence of childhood exposure to domestic violence, physical abuse, and sexual abuse approximately doubles the chances of both IPV perpetration and victimization by men in adulthood. Therefore, awareness of trauma and screening for adverse childhood experiences among these men is important for tailoring treatment (Voith et al., 2018).

The intersection of fatherhood and domestic violence is an increasing area of interest as programs in these fields have several underlying goals in common – such as fostering safe and healthy intimate partner and parent – child relationships – which strongly suggests that they would benefit from working together. However, it is common that advocates on either side do not know about the resources of the other. With a few significant exceptions, people working in the fields of domestic violence, healthy marriage, and responsible fatherhood have had very little to do with one another. Typically, they serve different populations and have a limited understanding of the experiences of each other's clients. They are largely unaware of each other's perspectives, breadth of activities, and areas of expertise (Ooms et al., 2006). When domestic violence survivors have concerns about services for their abusive partner or when fatherhood program staff express concern over fathers' descriptions of abusive or controlling behavior, they often do not know how to guide their clients or their own practice. The tension between helping families and holding offenders accountable is unavoidable but remains a barrier to fully coordinated interventions (Ferraro, 2017).

Battering intervention programs (BIPs) emerged in the United States in the late 1970s as one component of the social response to IPV. Most men in BIPs in the United States are mandated as a consequence of arrest for a crime related to domestic violence. Many men mandated to BIPs are first-time arrestees and do not engage in systematic coercive control of their partner (Ferraro, 2017). Battering intervention programs are also commonly known as *batterer* intervention programs. The term *battering* rather than *batterer* is preferred to emphasize that IPV is a behavior, not an intrinsic characteristic or identity of a person (Boggess & Groblewski, 2011).

BIPs and other IPV services reach a relatively small proportion of men, women, and families affected by IPV. Not all affected by IPV can access services even when mandated or required. Further, men, African American men in particular, can be difficult to reach (Boggess & Groblewski, 2011). Aymer (2011) and Waller (2016) argue that most BIPs are not inclusive of the experiences and needs of African American men, resulting in higher attrition. Because unemployment and low educational level may be crucial factors in explaining lower rates of attendance among many minority men, help in meeting basic material needs may be needed. Additionally, one of the first issues that needs to be addressed for men of color is their heightened resentment toward the criminal justice system – and society as a whole – for the racial discrimination they have suffered (Saunders, 2008). Although one catalyst for the creation of BIPs was victims' desires for treatment rather than punishment for abusers, BIPs are still closely linked with the criminal justice system. Many victims who wish to remain with their partners or are otherwise wary of formal institutions are suspicious of BIPs and accompanying services.

While most fathers who avail themselves of fatherhood programs' services are not batterers, these program representatives' experience and the aforementioned research indicate that IPV is of critical significance if programs are to serve fathers and families in healthy and holistic ways (Roulet, 2003). There have been many recommendations that fathering programs should be incorporated into BIPs to address fathers' violence toward their intimate partners as well as their children (Edleson, 1999; Scott, 2004). These recommendations are based on the premise that these programs are useful to combat child maltreatment while also combatting IPV. Employing different teaching strategies, these father-focused BIPs focus on different types of parenting skills and conflict management techniques to teach the men how to respond to conflict that occurs with the women and children in their lives. All father-focused BIPs have two primary objectives they seek throughout the course of the program: increasing accountability in violent fathers for the violent actions they commit and teaching positive fathering techniques in an effort to improve the father–child relationship (Labarre, Bourassa, Holden, Turcotte, & Letourneau, 2016). These programs are conducted with the primary goal of teaching the men why battering is wrong and how not to batter while still ensuring the safety of the women and the children that are in the men's lives (Martin, 2018).

In a recent national survey, 82% of the programs reported that most BIPs (>95%) embrace a group format. Group leaders generally believe that the group format has several advantages, including decreasing a sense of isolation, the opportunity for more realistic role plays, and the opportunity for feedback and confrontation from one's peers (Pirog-Good & Stets-Kealey, 1985). Evidence from qualitative studies indicates that African American men in same-race groups felt more cohesion than those in multirace groups (Saunders, 2008; Williams, 1998), but it was not clear if they had higher retention rates. Concerns have been raised recently about negative outcomes in groups, as group approaches can also make it difficult to individualize treatments and group dynamics can be difficult to handle with resistant clients (Murphy & Eckhardt, 2005).

Perhaps the greatest challenge in working with men who batter can be their lack of motivation for treatment (Daly & Pelowski, 2000). Motivational enhancement methods seem especially effective with minority clients (Taft, Murphy, Elliott, & Keaser, 2001). Motivational interviewing (MI), sometimes called motivation enhancing treatment (MET) is a strategy of intervention designed to reduce dropout and improve outcomes among clients who are reluctant to attend treatment and/or change their behavior (Miller & Rollnick, 2002). Developed in the spirit of the transtheoretical model, MI was also designed to facilitate movement through the stages of change (Miller & Rollnick, 2002). Therapists using MI or MET focus on four primary intervention techniques: (a) expressing empathy, (b) developing discrepancies between clients' current behaviors and desired outcomes, (c) rolling with resistance (or avoiding confrontation), and (d) supporting self-efficacy for change (Scott, King, McGinn, & Hosseini, 2011). Given that lack of motivation is an obstacle to treating men who have battered, combined with the documented success rates of MI with other populations, the application of MI in BIPs is a logical next step (Daniels & Murphy, 1997; Ganley, 1987; Murphy & Baxter, 1997). MI may be a useful model for addressing any denial issues because the goal is for them to become confronted with a discrepancy between what they believe/want and how they behave. Most men who use IPV do not believe in hitting women, yet their behavior suggests otherwise. The means by which denial is addressed by MI, however, is not one of direct confrontation, which is heavily relied upon by many BIPs. Rather, the client is invited to make the arguments for change; the therapist simply provides the direction (via the use of open-ended questions that invite change talk) and the atmosphere (i.e., one of unconditional positive regard) in which this can happen. Facilitators discuss men's ambivalence about change and encourage them to embrace the program as a way to reach their own goals (Ferraro, 2017). Further, MI may work in conjunction with men's tendency to solve problems independently because this approach emphasizes autonomy over one's decisions and behavior (Ganley, 1987; Kistenmacher & Weiss, 2008).

Practice

Carmen was a program instructor in an organization that provided evidence-based trauma-informed alternatives to prevailing punitive methods of working with domestic violence offenders. The program only serves men who had issues with their intimate partners. The fathers are usually court ordered to attend the program after being arrested for some form of IPV. However, many program participants are self-referred or are referred by word of mouth. The intake process usually takes about an hour and a half or two hours, and every participant has to go through a six-hour orientation. Some men are strictly on the fatherhood track, where they may be in the BIP and a fatherhood class. The majority of the fathers that Carmen served were young African American males. However, the men came from all different walks of life, from those who were homeless to those who had six-figure incomes and lived in the suburbs. Next to employment challenges, a "considerable" number of fathers come into the program with substance abuse and mental health issues. There is also a co-located mental health agency where men dealing with trauma recovery can receive mental health counseling.

While Carmen was self-employed as a national trainer for parent education facilitators, for three years, she, along with a male co-facilitator, worked with these fathers for six months, two hours per week on various topics such as objectifying women, relationships, and dealing with child abuse and neglect from their own childhood experiences. A curriculum is utilized, but the classes are not instructor directed. The clients take ownership of the group and instructors try to create as much small-group dialogue between the clients. Therefore, the richness and power of client change really comes from the diversity (i.e., age, education, income) in their group.

Case Study

The client is an African American male who is 25 years old with two daughters. He came in and he was so angry and borderline disrespectful during intake. Every time, he was asked a question he would say, "Well what do you think" or "How do you feel" and he had to keep being redirected. It was his way of trying to intimidate staff in the intake process. He was a challenge and initially did not want to sign the contract required for services. But then he came to class every Thursday morning and was so bright. He was able to embrace the concepts and process and internalize them in a way that no one else had done. He ended up being a volunteer with the local Fatherhood Summit. He started setting goals for himself because he was working jobs that he really didn't like and he set a goal for himself that he needed to have a job with benefits because he wanted to be able to take his kids to the doctor, get his medical care, and have real health insurance. We brainstormed with him and gave him a couple job leads. He wound up getting a job at Starbucks with benefits. He had a plan and followed it through. Next, he ended up getting an opportunity to go with the mayor and he ended up going to the state correctional institution to speak and motivate other men and he came back and was able to share that with the BIP group. Also, as a result of that experience, he went from a volunteer to one of the panel speakers at the local Fatherhood Summit. He was so empowered, and this situation will last him a lifetime.

Strategies

Reducing Bias

When meeting a client for the first time, to reduce any bias one might experience, it is critical to meet the client before reviewing his referral or court records. When a client first comes in, there is no discussion about the case because all of us are more than our behavior, which might be an isolated incident. Clients are asked to tell a little bit about themselves, not the person sent by the judge. Then they are asked to talk about the situation that brings them to the program, without any judging. We have the court records but do not read the records until after the men leave to prevent bias and judgment. It allows them to tell their side of the story.

Motivational Interviewing

Working with men is understanding that they have not always had opportunities to express themselves emotionally. Women find a way to get their emotional needs met—we call a mother, sister, or friend and share. Men are socialized in a way where they do not have a lot of outlets or support. But when they do, there are immediate positive outcomes. During the six-hour orientation with Carmen's program, a lot of the posturing and defenses come up because they just need to be able to release in a nonthreatening, noncompetitive situation. The tool of motivational interviewing helps the men to let those barriers down. Motivational interviewing begins in the intake process when men are asked to describe what brought them to the program. Prompts such as "Make me feel like I was there" and "Tell me what do you think happened from everybody's perspective" work at a rapid pace with this population because they usually don't have as many opportunities to share and not be judged or told what to do.

Redirecting

Some of the discussions that fathers bring up are very "raw" or "rough" in terms of their language or contain descriptions of domestic violence or anger towards the mother of their children. One of the challenges encountered in group was the language that the men use. Therefore, expectations are established on the front end. During the orientation, we state that it is not okay to refer to their partners as "girl" (e.g., "my girl this, my girl that"). While they do not really mean any offense, we try to help them see that there is a difference between a woman and a girl. We share that when they say girl, we assume that they are talking about somebody under 18. If they are not referring to a child, they should say woman, child's mother, or partner.

Lessons Learned

This work and specific case highlights some of the principles of effective treatment, which include matching the client's level of risk to the intensity of treatment, addressing the client's needs, delivering treatment to which the client will respond, and using treatment that is respectful and employs cognitive-behavioral and social learning methods (Ferraro, 2017). Respecting people, valuing them, and not judging their experience has been a thing to really help men change and sustain providers in this work. Additionally, the unique thing this BIP offered was allowing the staff to deal with the depth of the person—inside and out. This is very unique because a lot of social service agencies and funders are so driven by numbers and surveys and not the people and relationships. We wrapped all the community services around the fathers to prevent them from going door to door on their own for help. We empowered and embraced them in a way that they were willing to receive services. There is not a lack of resources, but these men do not feel that they have access to them and are not made to feel valued when they try to access the resources.

References

Appel, A.E., & Holden, G.W. (1998). The co-occurrence of spouse and physical child abuse: A review and appraisal. *Journal of Family Psychology*, 12, 578–599.

Aymer, S. (2011). A case for including the "lived experience" of African American men in batterers' treatment. *Journal of African American Studies*, 15(3), 352–356.

Boggess, J., & Groblewski, J. (2011). *Safety and services*. Retrieved from http://www.ncdsv. org/images/CFPP_SafetyServicesWomenOfColorSpeakAboutTheirCommunities_10-2011.pdf.

Bair-Merritt, M.H., Blackstone, M., & Feudtner, C. (2006). Physical health outcomes of childhood exposure to intimate partner violence: A systematic review. *Pediatrics*, 117(2), e278–290.

Daly, J.E., & Pelowski, S. (2000). Predictors of dropout among men who batter: A review of studies with implications for research and practice. *Violence and Victims*, 15, 137–160.

Edleson, J.L. (1999). The overlap between child maltreatment and woman battering. *Violence Against Women*, 5(2), 134–154. Retrieved from http://doi.org/10.1177/107780129952003.

Ferraro, K.J. (2017). Current research on batterer intervention programs and implications for policy. *Battered Women's justice project*. Retrieved from https://pdfs.semanticscholar.org/2212/7a108fa5f4fcea863dce9ced1f7fd6e529c2.pdf.

Gondolf, E. (2008). Outcomes of case management for African American men in batterer counseling. *Journal of Family Violence*, 23, 173–181.

Gondolf, E.W., & Williams, O.J. (2001). Culturally focused batterer counseling for African American men. *Trauma, Violence, & Abuse*, 2, 283–295.

Holden, G.W. (2003). Children exposed to domestic violence and child abuse: Terminology and taxonomy. *Clinical Child and Family Psychology Review*, 6(3), 151–160.

Karberg, E., Parekh, J., Scott, M.E., Areán, J.C., Kim, L., Laurore, J., & Bair-Merritt, M. (2020). *Preventing and Addressing Intimate Violence when Engaging Dads (PAIVED): Challenges, successes, and promising practices from responsible fatherhood programs*. Washington, DC: OPRE.

Kistenmacher, B.R., & Weiss, R.L. (2008). Motivational interviewing as a mechanism for change in men who batter: A randomized controlled trial. *Violence and Victims*, 23(5), 558–570.

Kitzmann, K.M., Gaylord, N.K., Holt, A.R., & Kenny, E.D. (2003). Child witnesses to domestic violence: A meta-analytic review. *Journal of Consulting and Clinical Psychology*, 71(2), 339–352.

Labarre, M., Bourassa, C., Holden, G.W., Turcotte, P., & Letourneau, N. (2016). Intervening with fathers in the context of intimate partner violence: An analysis of ten programs and suggestions for a research agenda. *Journal of Child Custody*, 13(1), 1–29. doi:10.1080/15379418.2016.1127793.

Martin, C.M. (2018). *The Incorporation of Fathering Interventions into Batterer Intervention Programs*. University Honors Theses. Paper 581. https://doi.org/10.15760/honors.590.

Miller, W.R., & Rollnick, S. (2002). *Motivational interviewing: Preparing people of change.* New York: Guildford Press.

Murphy, C., & Eckhardt, C. (2005). *Treating the abusive partner: An individualized cognitive behavioral approach.* New York: Guilford.

National Center for Injury Prevention and Control, Division of Violence Prevention. (2017a). *Intimate partner violence: Consequences.* Retrieved from https://www.cdc.gov/violenceprevention/intimatepartnerviolence/fastfact.html.

National Center for Injury Prevention and Control, Division of Violence Prevention. (2017b). *Intimate partner violence: Definitions.* Retrieved from https://www.cdc.gov/violenceprevention/intimatepartnerviolence/definitions.html.

Ooms, T., Boggess, J., Menard, A., Myrick, M., Roberts, P., Tweedie, J., & Wilson, P. (2006). *Building bridges between healthy marriage, responsible fatherhood, and domestic violence programs.* Washington, DC: Center for Law and Social Policy.

Pennell, J., Rikard, R.V., & Sanders-Rice, T. (2013). Family Violence: Fathers assessing and managing their risk to children and women. *Children and Youth Services Review,* 47, 36–45. doi:10.1016/j.childyouth.2013.11.004.

Pirog-Good, M., & Stets-Kealey, J. (1985). Male batterers and battering prevention programs: A national survey. *Response to the Victimization of Women & Children,* 8, 8–12.

Roulet, M. (2003). *Fatherhood programs and domestic violence. Center on Fathers, Families, and Public Policy.* Retrieved from https://cffpp.org/wp-content/uploads/TA_Fthd_DomViol.pdf.

Saunders, D.G. (2008). Group interventions for men who batter: A summary of program descriptions and research. *Violence and Victims,* 23(2), 156–172.

Saunders, D.G., & Parker, J.C. (1989). Legal sanctions and treatment follow-through among men who batter: A multivariate analysis. *Social Work Research & Abstracts,* 25(3), 21–29.

Scott, K., Heslop, L., Kelly, T., & Wiggins, K. (2015). Intervening to prevent repeat offending among moderate- to high-risk domestic violence offenders. *International Journal of Offender Therapy and Comparative Criminology,* 59(3), 273–294. doi:10.1177/0306624X13513709.

Scott, K.L. (2004). Predictors of change among male batterers: Application of theories and review of empirical findings. *Trauma, Violence, & Abuse,* 5(3), 260–284. doi:10.1177/1524838003264339.

Scott, K.L., & Crooks, C.V. (2006). Intervention for abusive fathers: Promising practices in court and community responses. *Juvenile and Family Court Journal,* 57(3), 29–44. doi:10.1111/j.1755-6988.2006.tb00126.x.

Scott, K.L., & Crooks, C.V. (2007). Preliminary evaluation of an intervention program for maltreating fathers. *Brief Treatment and Crisis Intervention,* 7(3), 224–238. doi:10.1093/brief-treatment/mhm007.

Scott, K., King, C., McGinn, H., & Hosseini, N. (2011). Effects of motivational enhancement on immediate outcomes of batterer intervention. *Journal of Family Violence,* 26(2), 139–149.

Taft, C.T., Murphy, C.M., Elliott, J.D., & Keaser, M.C. (2001). Race and demographic factors in treatment attendance for domestically abusive men. *Journal of Family Violence,* 16, 385–400.

Voith, L.A., Logan-Greene, P., Strodthoff, T., & Bender, A.E. (2018). *A paradigm shift in batterer intervention programming: A need to address unresolved trauma. Trauma, Violence, & Abuse,* 21(4), 691–705, 1524838018791268.

Waller, B. (2016). Broken fixes: A systematic analysis of the effectiveness of modern and postmodern interventions utilized to decrease IPV perpetration among Black males remanded to treatment. *Aggression and Violent Behavior*, 27, 42–49. doi:10.1016/j.avb.2016.02.003.

Wathen, C.N., & MacMillan, H.L. (2013). Children's exposure to intimate partner violence: Impacts and interventions. *Pediatrics & Child Health*, 18(8), 419–422.

Williams, O.J. (1998). Healing and confronting the African American male who batters. R. Carrillo & J. Tello Eds., *Family violence and men of color* (pp. 74–94). New York: Springer Publishing.

10 Engaging and Working with African American Fathers Experiencing Homelessness

Latrice Rollins and Tonya Boose

Introduction

Homelessness is a major public health problem that has received considerable attention from clinicians, researchers, administrators, and policymakers in recent years. In 2016, 550,000 individuals experienced homelessness in the United States (Tsai, 2018). Within this population, 70% are adult males. Additionally, veterans are more likely than the general civilian population to experience homelessness (Fargo et al., 2012; Slaven & Llorente, 2019). While veterans represent 8% of the U.S. population, in 2010, 17% of those experiencing homelessness were veterans. Nearly 50% of these veterans experience mental illness, and two-thirds meet the criteria for substance use disorders (Community Solutions 100,000 Homes Campaign, 2011).

Most minority groups in the United States experience homelessness at higher rates than Whites and therefore make up a disproportionate share of this population. Homelessness is challenging to study, and the story of African Americans and homelessness is often absent from the usual study of this population (Johnson, 2010). African Americans make up 13% of the general population, but more than 40% of those experiencing homelessness (National Alliance to End Homelessness, 2018). Additionally, 33.1% of veterans experiencing homelessness are African American, compared with 12.3% of the general veteran population (National Alliance to End Homelessness, 2018).

The relationship between homelessness and male parenting is rarely discussed in the professional discourse on family homelessness. Research shows that 41% of men who are experiencing homelessness are in fact parents and about 16% of sheltered families include a father (Burt et al., 1999; National Center on Family Homelessness, 2014; U.S. Census Bureau, 2014). However, fathers often are not allowed in shelters, as most are for women with children. Therefore, the family is often separated.

Service delivery and policy reforms concerning homelessness have largely excluded fathers and their children (Barker, Kolar, Mallett, McArthur, & Saunders, 2011). Homelessness among single father families is a growing phenomenon in our society. As the gap between wages and housing costs widen, more single father families are catapulted onto the streets. However, most of the social and shelter services available to parents are geared toward women with children, which inadvertently excludes custodial fathers (Amato & MacDonald, 2011; Bui & Graham, 2006; Hamer & Marchioro, 2002; Schindler & Coley, 2007; Paquette & Bassuk, 2011; Pruett, Cowan, Cowan, & Pruett, 2009). With more than 2.6 million households in America being headed by single fathers, gaining access to much needed services and resources must be reevaluated and adjusted to accommodate single-father households (Pew Research Center, 2013). Many single fathers with children have a difficult time finding shelters that take men with children and those who do accommodate them are sporadically located throughout our nation.

The findings of several studies show that many fathers experiencing homelessness face gender-related discriminations because of cultural expectations of men and stereotypical notions that men are innately incompetent to raise a happy and healthy child (Bui & Graham, 2006; Hamer & Marchioro, 2002; Schindler & Coley, 2007). Men experiencing homelessness are often thought of as free-floating individuals, almost dysfunctional in their autonomy and separation from family and the community. Rarely do people think of these men as being fathers intimately connected to their children, even when they are unable to provide housing for them.

There is a notable absence in the literature about fathers experiencing homelessness, the challenges they face, and how services may best respond to their needs (Barker et al., 2011). Research in the field of homelessness often explicitly or implicitly focuses on single men as the norm due to their greater visibility. It is noteworthy that within theory and practice, these men experiencing homelessness are seldom addressed as parents, which indicates a gender bias (Diebäcker, Arhant, & Harner, 2015).

Although services and policies addressing homelessness in the United States continue to expand, fathers experiencing homelessness remain an underserved subgroup (Barker et al., 2011; Ferguson & Morley, 2011; National Coalition for the Homeless, 2009a, 2009b; Robbers, 2010). Homelessness is a particularly complex issue that requires a multifaceted response from social service professionals if it is to be efficiently and successfully resolved for fathers, children, and families. (Rogers & Rogers, 2019). Single-father families or two-parent families who do not have a home have become a complex issue, and this complexity contributes to the lack of accessible services and lack of coordination among shelters, organizations, and government agencies to help families in need (Bassuk, 2010, p.498). Despite a slight increase in father-specific services, such as education and employment programming, barriers associated with accessing support services continue to be seen as an impediment to these fathers' ability to resolve their homeless status (Barrett-Rivera, Lindstrom, & Kerewsky, 2013; Castillo & Sarver, 2012; Ferguson & Morley, 2011; Paquette & Bassuk, 2011; Rogers & Rogers, 2019). Several studies alluded to gaps in the social services available to fathers experiencing homelessness, as well as to a lack of resources to meet fathers' needs even among services that work exclusively with fathers. For example, agencies provided support and services such as child support and employment assistance, but not visitation areas for these fathers to visit with their children (Rogers & Rogers, 2019). Additionally, homeless support services mainly concentrate on the restoration of independent living and rarely address psychosocial topics such as parenting.

Practice

Tonya is the director of the Veterans Program and Client Engagement Center at a homeless center, The Gateway Center (GWC). She encounters single fathers raising their kids, where the mom is not present in their child's life, has died, is incarcerated, or is just separated. There are also a number of men who have children who are above the age of 18. However, the population served is typically African American (86%) and in their mid-forties with children who are over the age of 18. Therefore, the majority of clients need encouragement to rebuild relationships if they struggle with homelessness or mental health or substance abuse issues. Because the clients may have some kind of strained relationship with their children, GWC has a partnership with the University for Parents that comes in weekly to help broker that relationship for the man and his children. For those who have children under the age of 18, University for Parents and case managers help them to build healthy relationships with their children's mothers.

Regarding housing, veterans get the majority of the housing vouchers. If a veteran comes in and he has a family or he wants to be reunited with his children, because the children and/or the wife or girlfriend are someplace else, the goal is for them to be together. Thus, families have more priority and there is more leeway with the veterans as opposed to the general client population of men experiencing homelessness.

When the intake is done, clients meet with the Gateway case manager once a week. If they have a substance abuse diagnosis, then they are connected to the treatment program through Veterans Affairs (VA). The case manager knows their psychologist, the psychiatrist, and their primary doctor. They meet with their VA representative twice a month. Then every six weeks, there is a staffing with the client. At that time, all come to the table to address any issues with attendance or compliance with doctor's orders. At that time, it is decided whether their time will be extended or if they will get a firm discharge date. Clients also receive random screenings, however, and depending on the circumstance second, third, and fourth chances are given.

VA community meetings are held every Wednesday. Guest speakers also include agencies that focus on fatherhood and parenting. Clients are also connected with employment, property managers, or housing. Employers come on site and talk to clients about applying for positions.

Schools also come because a lot of veterans are eligible for grants to attend classes or to receive certifications in areas such as maintenance, mechanical, air conditioning, or health care. Clients also receive help with their applications for VA or Social Security disability benefits. An actual point person comes and speaks directly with them to give them support with filling out their applications and they can also go to the office, fill out their paperwork, and receive help with that process. Clients also receive help with obtaining any documents that they may need – birth certificates, Social Security, military forms, etc.

The goals are income, mental health, substance abuse, and independent living. However, there are challenges to achieving these goals. To obtain permanent housing, the required documents (e.g., child's birth certificates, legal custody paperwork) are a challenge for fathers who just have joint custody. If fathers do not have full custody, they cannot receive a two-bedroom apartment with housing assistance. For families, there must be documentation for the children and the wife or girlfriend.

Additionally, child support is a challenge. There are clients who are working hard to pay their child support. However, part of the child support policy issue is, if they are behind, child support is legally allowed to take 52% of their income. Therefore, if fathers are experiencing this challenge, we connect them to the fatherhood program that is sponsored through the child support office. With the veterans, it is mandated that every client and every veteran that comes and is on child support, we recommend that they get a CDL license. However, if their driver's license is suspended because of child support, the fatherhood program connects with them to get them training and negotiate with their child support agent to release their license.

Case Studies

Working with African American fathers experiencing homelessness warrants a few examples because the situations are very diverse across this population. Here are three cases of fathers who were served:

Case #1

The client was an African American male with four children. He came from Texas and was homeless. His wife was living with an aunt with the four kids, but there was not enough room for him. He came to the shelter to seek services. He had been homeless for about four or five months. When asked the question about the children, he did admit that there were some domestic violence issues with him and his wife at that time. They were separating and so he was doing a fresh start in Georgia. He definitely wanted to have his children to come visit him. He did get a job as security and started working the night shift. We referred him to the fatherhood program, but for whatever reason, they never connected him. He started calling the children, him and

the wife talked, and they decided that they wanted to work on their relationship. She had family here in Georgia, so she brought the kids to
Georgia. Then we got them connected with counseling at the VA. When it
was decided that they wanted to be a unit again, he came back to us to let us
know because we had already referred him to supportive services. Now, we
had to revisit the issue because he wanted to be reunited with his wife and his
kids. Because it was an intact family, he was eligible, and we were able to give
him a housing voucher from the VA. With the voucher, the wife come in
and provided her documentation – her birth certificate and the children's and
a printout of her income. There was no income at the time besides Social
Security. We got the children over to Fulton County so that they could get
registered for school and we submitted all the paperwork. When we had our
team meetings, the wife would come and then she would get the same
service that we had for her husband. While we were in case management
with her, she would meet with the client's case manager to make sure the
documentation was submitted and we were able to house them as a family.
His name, her name, and the children's names are on the lease. That is a
priority – keeping the family together, getting them housed, and putting
children in school.

Case # 2

The client was an African American father who had a daughter that he had
not seen in years, and she was in the military. They ended up getting back
in contact with each other and then he came to our center. He is very,
very articulate. He was a former accountant before things kind of fell apart
for him. It was funny getting him to work because, of course, with the
experience, his resume was so intimidating, and he was going for these
maintenance positions. He had an interview with Coca-Cola, and they
were so impressed with him. But he had to work his way up. It took a
minute, but he was very open. He took the clerk position in the accounting office. When he left us, he emailed me about a month later
because he had submitted his application to the county government for an
accounting job. He got the position and he emailed me to let me know
with his title. Meanwhile, his daughter came out of the military and she
was 21. He said, "My daughter is leaving the military and she needs a
place to stay." He was very vocal about needing a two-bedroom apartment and the VA gave him a hard time because she was 21. Someone got
in contact with her commander and confirmed that his daughter was
overseas at the time. When she got back to the States, she was adamant
that she wanted to live with her dad. Eventually, the VA finally agreed to
it and she came to live with him in a two-bedroom apartment. They had
been estranged for a while, so they were definitely open to counseling.
It has been over a year; he keeps in contact regularly, and he and his
22-year-old daughter are doing fine.

Case #3

The client is an African American father of one 13-year-old son. He came in and his wife had substance abuse issues. He had been clean for about six to seven months. However, she was not ready to deal with her issues. Because they were married, she had access to all the services that he has as his wife. But she was not ready. We had that real conversation with him about jeopardizing his housing and losing his child because of her substance abuse. He insisted that they were going to be okay and were going to be a family. We put in their paperwork, starting the process, and got him connected to services. After his last treatment, he came to us and he said his wife cannot move in because he had to come the realization that she was not going to stop using substances. We had to go back and make sure that her name was taken off the lease and her paperwork was given back to her. Of course, she was not happy, and she was aggressive, so we had the conversation with him about what he would do if she came to his door. Would he let her in? We did find out later that he did let her in, and he came home from work and it was a mess. He did put her out, because he was not going to risk losing his 13-year-old or the housing. He told her, when you are ready to get help, we will be here. But until then, you cannot be a part of this. She is remarried now. If she wants services, she is welcome to access them. She will get connected, but she has to want it. Currently, though, the services are just for him and his son, and they are doing fine.

Strategies

Assessment and Referral

When working with African American men who are experiencing homelessness, it is critical to first ask, do you have children? Often, men are not asked this question. Then there are differentiating responses to fathers who are homeless. Fathers have diverse experiences of parenting while homeless and services may need to respond to fathers differently depending on what they need to support their parenting. For example, Barker et al. (2011) suggest the following:

- Fathers who have no contact with the children may need support to reconnect. This may include services assisting in the writing of a letter to children or actively linking fathers to family counseling.
- Fathers who have contact may require a safe place to see their children. There is a serious need for more father/family–friendly places to support relationships.
- Fathers may require support for their parenting, active linking to child care and schools, and advocating for or navigating other services.

Rates of mental health and substance abuse disorders among minorities belonging to high-need subgroups, including persons experiencing homelessness, are disproportionately higher than among non-minorities (Substance Abuse and Mental Health Services Administration, 2003; U.S. Department of Health and Human Services, 2001). Compared to their White counterparts, minorities are less likely to receive adequate mental health and substance abuse care (Grella & Stein 2006; U.S. Department of Health and Human Services, 2001; Wells, Klap, Koike, & Sherbourne, 2001). Motivational interviewing has been found to be effective with substance abusing individuals experiencing homelessness (deLeon et al., 2011; Kennedy et al., 2018). Many of the conversations with the clients at the center involve motivational interviewing.

Additionally, when working with African American fathers who are experiencing homelessness, the first goal is to get them connected with services. Wraparound services or holistic approaches to service delivery are essential for providing comprehensive support to these fathers. Wraparound services are a vital component of support, especially given the complex nature of both homelessness and parenting (Cook-Craig & Koehly, 2011; Rogers & Rogers, 2019). We want them to be compliant with remaining clean if they have a substance abuse issue or adhering to their medication regime if they have a mental health issue. If they are interested in re-engaging with their children, we start off with them engaging for an hour or so a day with the child before they just jump to full custody. When mental health and substance abuse is involved, it just takes on a whole other level. Before he can be there for his kids or pay child support, he has to take care of himself. Therefore, needs are assessed during intake and treatment is recommended accordingly. Additionally, communication and interprofessional collaboration to ensure services are meeting the clients' needs are critical.

Group Work

The group aspect for working with men, specifically fathers, and helping them build those relationships is really positive. Clients at the center have provided positive feedback about participating in groups, specifically the University for Parents groups, because they get to see another man who is done it in the same group as them. It is really powerful, encouraging, and healthy for them.

Lessons Learned

There are several lessons learned that can be shared with students or practitioners who will work with this population. Practitioners have to be realistic. Sometimes, tough subjects have to be addressed because homelessness brings up a lot of emotions, such as shame and guilt, for African American fathers. This is a part of case management – having tough conversations with them and encouraging them to keep trying. They may be resistant to the conversation, but practitioners have to be persistent and keep trying to see where they are coming from. For example, a lot of the clients come in and say they want their child. Practitioners have to look at the big picture. Realistically speaking, we have to assess if there are substance or mental health issues and let them know they have to deal with their own issues first.

Practitioners also have to have an open mind; these fathers need the benefit of the doubt. There are so many systems and structures in society and programs that are against them or not for them. Also, having an open mind because as we demonstrated in one of the cases, it is never too late for a father and his children, even his adult children. Practitioners also need to know what services are available and realize they are going to have to work a little bit harder to find and obtain services because there is not as many for this population of fathers.

References

Amato, F., & MacDonald, J. (2011). Examining risk factors for homeless men: Gender role conflict, help-seeking behaviors, substance abuse and violence. *The Journal of Men's Studies*, 19, 227–235. https://doi.org/10.3149/jms.1903.227.

Barker, J., Kolar, V., Mallett, S., McArthur, M., & Saunders, V. (2011). More than just me: supporting fathers who are homeless, *Canberra*. Australia: Australian Catholic University.

Barrett-Rivera, B., Lindstrom, L., & Kerewsky, S. (2013). Parenting in poverty: The experiences of fathers who are homeless. *Journal of Human Services*, 33(1), 73–84.

Bassuk, E.L. (2010). Ending child homelessness in America. *American Journal of Orthopsychiatry*, 80, 496–504. doi:10.1111/j.1939-0025.2010.01052.x.

Bui, B. H., & G. Graham (2006). *Support issues for homeless single fathers and their Children*. Victoria University, Melbourne. Retrieved from http://static1.1.sqspcdn. com/static/f/929640/14202835/1316316123397/Single_Fathers_Homelessness. pdf?token=hXcPDMmSEmomLEiBnWzR0ClrZpA%3D.

Burt, M.R., Aron, L.Y., Douglas, T., Valente, J., Lee, E., & Iwen, B. (1999). *Homelessness: Programs and the people they serve*. Washington, DC: Urban Institute.

Castillo, J. T., & Sarver, C. M. (2012). Nonresident fathers' social networks: The relationship between social support and father involvement. *Personal Relationships*, 19, 759–774. https://doi.org/10.1111/j.1475-6811.2011.01391.x.

Community Solutions 100,000 Homes Campaign. (2011). *Data report: National survey of homeless veterans in 100,000 .homes*. Retrieved from https://www.va.gov/homeless/docs/nationalsurveyofhomelessveterans_final.pdf.

Cook-Craig, P., & Koehly, L. (2011). Stability in the social support networks of homeless families in shelter: Findings from a study of families in a faith-based shelter program. *Journal of Family Social Work*, 14, 191–207.

Culhane, D.P., Khadduri, J., Cortes, A., Buron, L., Leopold, J., Montgomery, A.E., & Kuhn, J. (2011). *Veteran homelessness: A supplemental report to the 2009 Annual Homeless Assessment Report to Congress*. Washington, DC: Abt. Associates and the US Department of Veterans Affairs National Center on Homelessness Among Veterans.

de León, X.Y.P., Amodei, N., Hoffman, T. J., Martinez, R., Treviño, M., & Medina, D. (2011). Real world implementation of an adapted ACT model with minority and non-minority homeless men. *International Journal of Mental Health and Addiction*, 9(6), 591–605.

Diebäcker, M., Arhant, Y., & Harner, R. (2015). Parenting within homelessness: A qualitative study on the situation of homeless fathers and social work in homeless support services in Vienna. *European Journal of Homelessness*, 9(2), 87.

Ferguson, S., & Morley, P. (2011). Improving engagement in the role of father for homeless, noncustodial fathers: A program evaluation. *Journal of Poverty*, 15, 206–225. https://doi.org/10.1080/10875549.2011.563175.

Grella, C.E., & Stein, J.A. (2006). Impact of program services on treatment outcomes of patients with comorbid mental and substance use disorders. *Psychiatric Services*, 57, 1007–1015.

Hamer, J., & Marchioro, K. (2002). Becoming custodial dads: Exploring parenting among low-income and working class African American fathers. *Journal of Marriage and the Family*, 64(1), 116–129. Retrieved from http://www.jstor.org/stable/3599781.

Hill, T. (2016). *Inclusiveness: Addressing the needs of homeless single fathers with children.* Retrieved from https://www.researchgate.net/profile/Tamara_Raymond-Hill/publication/305730578_Inclusiveness_Addressing_the_Needs_of_Homeless_Single_Fathers_with_Children/links/579e398108ae6a2882f53b5f/Inclusiveness-Addressing-the-Needs-of-Homeless-Single-Fathers-with-Children.

Johnson, R.A. (2010). African Americans and homelessness: moving through history. *Journal of Black Studies*, 40(4), 583–605.

Kennedy, D.P., Osilla, K.C., Hunter, S.B., Golinelli, D., Hernandez, E.M., & Tucker, J.S. (2018). A pilot test of a motivational interviewing social network intervention to reduce substance use among housing first residents. *Journal of Substance Abuse Treatment*, 86, 36–44.

National Alliance to End Homelessness (2018). *Racial inequalities in homelessness, by the numbers.* Retrieved from https://endhomelessness.org/resource/racial-inequalities-homelessness-numbers/.

National Alliance to End Homelessness (2010). *Racial inequalities in homelessness, by the numbers.* Washington DC: National Alliance to End Homelessness.

National Center on Family Homelessness. (2014). *America's youngest outcasts: State report card on child homelessness.* Newton, MA. Retrieved from https://tandfde.mpslimited.com/DigiEditPro/DigiEditPage.aspx?FileName=841169200852053.xml: Author. http://www.homelesschildrenamerica.org/

Paquette, K., & Bassuk, E. (2011). Beyond shelter doors: Fathers and homelessness. In C. H. Leyton, *Fatherhood: Roles, responsibilities & rewards* (93–101). Nova Science Publishers, Incorporated. Retrieved from http://www.center4si.com/Uploads/files/BeyondShelterDoors.pdf.

Pew Research Center. (2013). *The rise of single fathers: A ninefold increase since 1960.* Washington, DC: Author. Retrieved from http://www.pewsocialtrends.org/2013/07/02/the-rise-of-single-fathers/.

Pruett, M., Cowan, C., Cowan, P.A., & Pruett, K. (2009). Lessons learned from the Supporting Father Involvement study: A cross-cultural preventive intervention for low-income families with young children. *Journal of Social Service Research*, 35, 163–179. https://doi.org/10.1080/01488370802678942.

Robbers, M. (2010). Hispanic young fathers: An overview of programs and practices. *Childhood Education*, 86, 394–398.

Rogers, T.N., & Rogers, C.R. (2019). Social services professionals' views of barriers to supporting homeless noncustodial fathers. *Family Relations*, 68(1), 39–50.

Schindler, H.S., & Coley, R.L. (2007). A qualitative study of homeless fathers: Exploring parenting and gender role transitions. *Family Relations*, 56(1), 40–51. doi:10.1111/j.1741-3729.2007.00438.x.

Slaven, K., & Llorente, M.D. (2019). Homeless veterans and mental health, *Veteran Psychiatry in the US* (pp. 233–240). Cham: Springer.

Substance Abuse and Mental Health Services Administration. (2003). *Blueprint for change: Ending chronic homelessness for persons with serious mental illnesses and co-occurring substance use disorders*. Rockville: Center for Mental Health Services, Substance Abuse and Mental Health Services Administration.

Tsai, J. (2018). Lifetime and 1-year prevalence of homelessness in the U.S. population: Results from the National Epidemiologic Survey on Alcohol and Related Conditions-III. *Journal of Public Health*, 40(1), 65–74. http://dx.doi.org/10.1093/pubmed/fdx034.

Tsai, J., O'Toole, T., & Kearney, L.K. (2017). Homelessness as a public mental health and social problem: New knowledge and solutions. *Psychological Services*, 14(2), 113.

U.S. Census Bureau, (2014). *America's families and living arrangements: Family groups*. Table FG5. Washington D.C. Retrieved from https://www.census.gov/hhes/families/data/cps2014.html.

U.S. Department of Health and Human Services. (2001). *Mental Health: Culture, race and ethnicity—A supplement to mental health: A report of the surgeon general*. Rockville: U.S. Department of Health and Human Services, Public Health Service, Office of the Surgeon General.

Wells, K., Klap, R., Koike, A., & Sherbourne, C. (2001). Ethnic disparities in unmet need for alcoholism, drug Abuse, and mental health care. *American Journal of Psychiatry*, 158, 2027–2032.

11 Conclusion

Moving to Father-Inclusive Services

Latrice Rollins

Introduction

Father involvement can be supported at various levels within an organization depending on its goals. Father awareness is the first level of involvement, which involves educating staff about healthy fatherhood, addressing negative stereotypes about father involvement, and promoting a positive understanding that father involvement is complementary to and supportive of mother involvement. Father-friendliness is the second level and involves practices that consider fathers in service delivery and practice environment. These organizations are comfortable spaces for fathers to be involved in services. Father-inclusive organizations are the ultimate goal and have programming that meets the specific needs of men. In these organizations, "all fathers have equal and fair access to the support provided by high quality family services regardless of income, employment status, special educational needs or ethnic/language background" (Family Action Centre, 2008, p. 7). This framework occurs when the needs of fathers are responded to through planning and delivery of services. Furthermore, these organizations embrace an asset- or strengths-based approach and recognize "fathers' aspirations for their children's well-being and the experience, knowledge and skills they contribute to this well-being" (Family Action Centre, 2008, p. 7).

Based on the research and practice experience shared in this book that demonstrates that African American fathers want to be engaged, and their engagement leads to positive outcomes, it is important for organizations to move towards father-inclusive practice, if they haven't already. There are several competencies that are needed to prepare for and implement father-inclusive practice or research and they fall into three domains: knowledge, skills, and mindset.

Themes of Engagement and Practice with African American Fathers

The engagement strategies and lessons learned across the cases in each chapter were analyzed, and five themes that characterized these professionals work with African American fathers were found:

Knowledge	Skills	Mindset
• Historical discourse of father involvement • Parental roles • Fatherhood research and theories • Power dynamics	• Cultural humility & competence • Communication • Engagement • Participatory strategies • Resource brokering/service navigation • Interprofessional collaboration	• Aware of self & others • Strengths perspective • Ethical • Professional

Figure 11.1 Father Competency Framework.

- Theme 1: Relationship
- Theme 2: Motivational Interviewing
- Theme 3: Group Work
- Theme 4: Wraparound Services
- Theme 5: Trauma

These themes, including the competencies needed for father-inclusive practice, are described in detail below.

Theme 1: Relationship

Every chapter author shared how important it was to establish a trusting, genuine helping relationship with the fathers. Mazza (2002) found that when African American fathers feel respected, liked, and wanted, they are very willing to enter into helping relationships. Vann (2007) also stated the key to engagement is staff who can form a true connection with fathers in their community. An important step in building the helping relationship with African American fathers is to build empathy. For a group that often is dehumanized and negatively stereotyped, empathy matters. Trout (2010) states that empathy can be defined as mercy and an empathic reaction such as compassion is the emotion we feel for the misery of others when we either see it or are made to conceive it in a very lively manner. Further, Trout (2010) defines empathy as the capacity to accurately understand the position of others – to feel that "this could happen to me." Empathy enables staff to take the perspective of the fathers they serve.

An empathy exchange between the staff and the fathers is the foundation for engagement but must be accompanied by action (Ginwright, 2018; Trout, 2010). Empathy increases the awareness of others' suffering, but it is not clear that empathy motivates or prevents individuals to act (Brooks, 2011). This is especially true when acting may cost the individual or go against a prevailing code or norm. The norm in most agencies is to focus on the mother and/or the child. The chapter authors demonstrated that African American female fatherhood service providers can engage and are motivated to work with African American fathers because they not only feel for the fathers they serve, they were compelled to act by a sense of duty (Brooks, 2011). Empathic staff working with African American fathers must find ways of moving to action even in the face of intense obstacles that the fathers face or that they may face within their organizations (Brooks, 1999). Despite some challenges, the women did not express difficulty establishing relationships with fathers or meeting their needs.

Theme 2: Motivational Interviewing

Several of the chapter authors described the use of motivational interviewing with African American fathers as a best practice. Motivational interviewing (MI) is well documented in the literature as an effective approach with those recovering from substance abuse or addiction, and it appears to be particularly effective for individuals who are initially not ready to change (Butler et al., 1999; Heather, Rollnick, Bell, & Richmond, 1996; Miller & Rollnick, 1991; Miller, 1996; Resnicow, Jackson, Wang, Dudley, & Baranowski, 2001; Rollnick & Miller, 1995; Resnicow et al., 2002). Increasingly, this approach has also been found to be effective with African American men and fathers. Therefore, staff should be proficient with MI (Clark, 2005). Using MI techniques early can enhance fathers' initial motivation to achieve healthy goals and build rapport in the helping relationship (Rostad, Self-Brown, Boyd, Osborne, & Patterson, 2017). MI recognizes and accepts that fathers who need to make changes in their lives are at different levels of readiness to do so (Levinsky, Forcehimes, O'Donohue, & Beitz, 2007; Shannon & Abrams, 2007).

Miller and Rollnick (2002) describe MI as a client-centered approach for eliciting behavior change by helping clients to explore and resolve ambivalence. It helps individuals to work through their ambivalence about behavior change and allows the staff to tailor the content and format of the encounter to match the participant's readiness to change, subjective pros and cons for change, and level of efficacy. It is a method to facilitate and reinforce intrinsic motivation within individuals to change their behavior (Martinez et al., 2013). MI is not a discrete intervention strategy but a combination of several principles and techniques drawn from several theoretical perspectives. Key techniques used in MI include listening reflectively and eliciting self-motivational statements.

MI is client centered, in that the staff attempt to understand the client's expectations, beliefs, perspectives, and concerns about changing his behaviors. During the encounter, the client is expected to do most of the work with the facilitation and guidance by the staff. The staff is an engaged problem-solving partner rather than an aloof, omniscient provider of information, advice, and counsel (Rollnick & Miller, 1995; Rogers, 1986). Interventions are calibrated to the client's level of readiness to change, with educational approaches given only when the patient is ready and willing to hear the information and provided in a collaborative, autonomy-promoting manner. Unlike many traditional counseling approaches, MI rarely involves providing information or advice unless the client requests it. Providing education to clients who are ambivalent about change has paradoxical effects, producing resistance to change (Boardman, Catley, Grobe, Little, & Ahluwalia, 2006; Miller, Benefield, & Tonigan, 1993; Moyers & Martin, 2006).

The tone of the encounter is positive, encouraging, empathetic, and nonconfrontational. MI staff avoid arguments and "roll with resistance" rather than contest it. MI is directive in that the conversation is structured to produce movement toward change. A comfortable and nonjudgmental atmosphere is created that allows the client to talk about the pros and cons of changing, without coercion to change or premature suggestions of change options. The core of MI involves strengthening intrinsic motivation by discussing how change is consistent with the client's own values and goals. Clients make their own decisions about change, which has been shown to increase commitment to change (Borrelli, Tooley, & Scott-Sheldon, 2015). MI concepts may also be used to tailor the delivery of the intervention to facilitate desired behaviors (Allport et al., 2018).

Theme 3: Group Work

Most evaluation studies document that group work is a major component of responsible fatherhood programs (The Lewin Group, 1997; United States Department of Health and Human Services, 2003). Many of the chapter authors described facilitating groups with African American fathers or working with fathers who participated in groups in their organizations. Some chapter authors described African American fathers' desire to be a part of a support group, but there were none available or offered. It is evident from these cases that staff should employ more group interventions to meet the personal and interpersonal needs of African American fathers. Therefore, staff seeking to engage African American fathers should be prepared for practice with groups (Hopps & Pinderhughes, 1999). Genuineness, commitment, and personal comfort along with professional skill are essential group leader attributes that have been found to be effective with this population regardless of the leader's gender, as demonstrated in our chapter authors' cases (Franklin, 1999; Rollins, 2010).

Group work is a way to engage African American fathers if presented in a male-friendly manner that affirms his strengths. Further, group work allows staff to earn their trust and delve into topics they might not otherwise explore (Shallcross, 2010; Sutton; 1996). It is also effective to organize African American fathers into positive, healthy relationships (Sturdivant & Byrdsong, 2013). Groups for African American fathers can provide them an opportunity to change conventional ways of relating to each other and encourage a different kind of fraternal support built on better ways of using each other and the community to change their life circumstance (Franklin, 1999).

Group work can serve as a special outlet for discussing common feelings and thoughts about being an African American father. To engage fathers, staff should emphasize the informality of the group process and structure the groups as typical conversational exchanges among African American men. Framing the groups as a forum to discuss life as well as appealing to the need to restructure the way that African American fathers communicate with each other can reduce their typical resistance to these therapy-like situations (Franklin, 1999). Groups can assist African American fathers understand and balance external social factors, such as racism, and internal psychological factors, such as disillusionment and self-doubt (Franklin, 1999). While men tend to avoid the stigma of engaging in therapy, they enjoy the opportunity to communicate with, and learn from, others facing similar issues with their partners, children, and parents as they try to fulfill their cultural roles as protectors and providers. Some evidence suggests that men are more likely to engage with other men in fathering programs and prefer men-only programs (Pruett, Pruett, Cowan, & Cowan, 2017). Men-only services will likely draw younger men (e.g., teenage dads) and those developing their own identities and roles and parents in conflict (Pruett et al., 2017). Group work can also help to manage the stress of being treated like an invisible man (Franklin, 1999). Fathers, especially African American fathers, often share that they feel ignored, or invisible to staff.

Theme 4: Wraparound Services

Research studies have found that fathers will participate in services, if given the opportunity and if the service meets their needs (Julion, Gross, Barclay-McLaughlin, & Fogg, 2007; Roy, 2008). The chapter authors described adjusting service plans to meet the needs of the fathers. Franklin (2010) agreed that when working with African American fathers, "[N]o one approach was as sacred as was adaptability to the circumstances of the needs of the clients in the counseling process" (p. 137). Programs for fathers where only education and employment assistance are provided are considered outdated. Programs now offer anger management, intensive therapy, substance abuse counseling, relationship skills, and parent education. These programs are beginning to move away from what Hopps, Pinderhughes, and Shankar (1995) describe as the "deviant pathological or equivalence opportunity paradigm" (p. 70).

While these programs still include components that require fathers to improve their individual character, the chapter authors demonstrated an understanding of the impact of institutional and structural forces on the fathers' lives. Therefore, several of the programs were set up as "one-stop shops" where staff often addressed parenting, child support, employment, mental health, and substance abuse within one program. Further, many of the chapter authors stated that they worked with fathers so that they could take action themselves against many of the institutions, such as the criminal justice, child support, and educational systems, that negatively impact them, their children and families, and community.

These chapter authors also demonstrated the need for integrated or coordinated care. Many agencies are serving the same families (Hodgkinson, 1992), and the professional responsibility for specific services is often uncoordinated and dysfunctional. An increasing number of federal and state policymakers and legislators now recognize that a systemic, collaborative approach across child and family serving organizations is imperative. The Administration for Children and Families (ACF) issued a joint information memorandum (IM), Integrating Approaches that Prioritize and Enhance Father Engagement, emphasizing the importance of meaningful father engagement in all ACF programs to better serve children and families. While several of these memorandums have been issued previously, the new addition to this IM was the request that agencies work together across governments to jointly create and maintain an environment that prioritizes father engagement as a critical factor in strengthening families. The National Commission on Leadership in Interprofessional Educational (NCLIE) generated five positions:

1. Families are needed as partners in improving the preparation programs that train service providers and as partners in improving service delivery systems.
2. Each program is unique and must emerge from the cultural setting in which it will operate and be planned by the people who will make it work.
3. Families must be involved in developing the plans to improve their neighborhoods to have a sense of ownership in these plans and sustain them over time.
4. The primary job of service providers is to create the conditions for change. Their primary goal is to enable families to act on their own behalf.
5. A shared vision of the future is what will bring families and professionals together (Corrigan & Bishop, 1997).

These principles would encourage father-inclusive practice. To move from principles to practice, the infrastructures supporting health and human service professions should be redesigned to promote more efficient and effective systems of care. At all levels, we must invest in and ensure that all systems collaborate to address African American fathers' needs (Rich, 2016).

In addition to the infrastructure, collective effectiveness is determined by the degree of collaboration among professionals that can be achieved (Bauwens & Hourcade, 1995; Friend & Cook, 2000; Lim & Adelman, 1997; Thomas, Correa, & Morsink, 1995; Tourse, Mooney, Kline, & Davoren, 2005). Interprofessional collaboration is essential for staff across programs and systems to engage and work with African American fathers. Increasingly, it is recognized that not only organizational structures need to change but also the skills and orientation of professionals (Brandon & Knapp, 1999). Historically, professionals from diverse disciplines have been used in a parallel, rather than a collaborative, process (Allen-Meares, 1996; Allen-Meares, Washington, & Welsh, 1996; Ginsburg, 1989; O'Callaghan, 1993; Tourse & Sulick, 1999). Traditional professional preparation for those who engage African American fathers and their families focuses on the development of understandings, beliefs, and skill sets that relate to the knowledge base of each discipline. One innovative, constructive, and effective means of preparation is to jointly train professionals from different professions, such as criminal justice, education, health, and social work, in collaborative practice (Tourse et al., 2005).

Theme 5: Trauma

Trauma disproportionately affects the lives of African American fathers. Several of the chapter authors recognized that they had to work with their clients to address traumatic experiences. Trauma can take a physiological and psychological toll. The impact of childhood adversity and unrelenting stress (also known as "toxic stress") on future chronic disease and the early deaths of African American men are well documented (Courtenay, 2011; Griffith, Bruce, & Thorpe Jr, 2019). These men are more likely to suffer toxic stresses imposed by chronic poverty, racism, unconscious bias, and the brutality at the hands of the police and other human-serving systems. Unfortunately, there has been a lack of a healing response from the many systems (e.g., health care, mental health, public health, law enforcement, social services) who ideally are to serve African American fathers. In fact, these systems often re-traumatize and dehumanize them when they engage with these systems. There is clear evidence that within multiple systems, African American fathers are viewed as responsible for any negative situations they experience. Only with this understanding can staff engage and work with African American fathers effectively and effect the fundamental system transformation necessary to ensure equity and healing for them to realize their fullest potential. There are several approaches to addressing trauma with African American fathers. Below is a brief summary of three approaches – trauma-informed care, healing-centered engagement, and post-traumatic growth – that can be implemented according to the fathers' needs.

Trauma results from substantial negative experience(s) imposed directly on a person and relates to what happens around them in their families, communities, and the broader society (Rich, 2016). Trauma as experienced by African American fathers is unique in historical context and in its manifestation in contemporary American society. The history of the African American father in America is a history of trauma (e.g., separating families during slavery, lynchings, police brutality). Psychological trauma is the unique individual experience of a singular event or persistent conditions, in which the individual's ability to integrate his/her emotional experience is overwhelmed or the individual experiences a threat to life, body/person, or sanity (Pearlman & Saakvitne, 1995; Simpson & Starky, 2006). A traumatic event or situation can overwhelm an individual's ability to cope, leaving that person fearing death, annihilation, mutilation, or psychosis. Sturdivant and Byrdsong (2013) state that the circumstances of the event can include abuse of power, betrayal of trust, entrapment, helplessness, pain, confusion, and/or loss. There are both individual and collective traumatic experiences. African American men (and women) across the country vicariously experienced the trauma of the killings of Ahmaud Arbery, Breonna Taylor, George Floyd, and countless others.

Sturdivant and Byrdsong (2013) propose an African-centered approach to address trauma, which embraces the terms Maafa (a state of woundedness) and Ma'at (a state of health and wellness. The act of Maafa requires the denial of the validity of African people's humanity and is manifested in an enduring total disregard and disrespect for our right to exist. Maafa is the perpetuation of systemic and organized processes of psychological, spiritual, and physical destruction of people of African descent, which is especially true for African American fathers. Ma'at consists of 42 negative confessions and seven cardinal virtues: truth, justice, rightness, harmony, balance, reciprocity, and order (Walker, 2010). By acknowledging trauma (Maafa), allowing for the expression of trauma and guiding the individual through self-directed solutions, wellness (Ma'at) is achieved (Sturdivant & Byrdsong, 2013).

Trauma-informed care broadly refers to a set of principles that guide and direct how we view the impact of severe harm on individual's health. Trauma-informed care encourages support and treatment to the whole person, rather than focusing on only treating individual symptoms or specific behaviors. The assumption is that negative behaviors are the symptom of a deeper harm, rather than willful deviance, defiance, or disrespect. While there is a growing field of research related to trauma-informed care (Bath, 2008; Ko et al., 2008), it is limited in its presumption that trauma is an individual experience rather than a collective one and provides little insight into how to address the root cause of trauma (Ginwright, 2018). By only treating the individual, the toxic systems, policies, and practices that traumatize individuals are left unchanged (Ginwright, 2018).

A healing-centered approach (HCE) is holistic, involving culture, spirituality, civic action, and collective healing. HCE views trauma not simply as an individual isolated experience but rather highlights the ways in which trauma and healing are experienced collectively. HCE addresses trauma by moving beyond "what happened to you" to "what's right with you" and views those exposed to trauma as agents in the creation of their own well-being rather than victims of traumatic events. Healing-centered approaches are asset- or strengths-based and de-center trauma (Wilson & Richardson, 2020). Staff should be trauma informed and healing centered. Ginwright (2018) describes the framework for healing-centered engagement:

1. HCE is explicitly political, rather than clinical – trauma and well-being as function of the environments where people live, work, and play. When people advocate for policies and opportunities that address causes of trauma, these activities contribute to a sense of purpose, power, and control over life situations
2. HCE is culturally grounded and views healing as the restoration of identity. It highlights the intersectional nature of identity and highlights the ways in which culture offers a shared experience, community, and sense of belonging. Healing is experienced *collectively* and is shaped by shared identity such as race, gender, and/or sexual orientation.
3. HCE is asset driven and focuses on well-being we want rather than symptoms we want to suppress; it builds upon clients' experiences, knowledge, skills, and curiosity as positive traits to be enhanced.
4. HCE supports staff with their own healing with structures like team retreats for employees or creating incentives like continuing education units for deeper learning about well-being and healing.

Finally, researchers begun to systematically study and theorize the phenomenon of positive change following traumatic life events, now commonly called post-traumatic growth (PTG), as a resiliency-based approach to addressing trauma, including race-based trauma (Tedeschi & Calhoun, 1995). An alternative to post-traumatic stress disorder (PTSD), PTG acknowledges the resilience and growth that can occur after trauma (Calhoun, Cann, Tedeschi, & McMillan, 2000; Van Slyke, 2013). Researchers purported that between 30% and 90% of individuals who have experienced trauma reported positive growth and change (Sawyer & Ayers, 2009). PTG is often thought to occur after a traumatic event significant enough to challenge an individual's previous assumptions about the world (i.e., victim or witness of violent event such as sexual assault, interpersonal violence, natural disaster) (Larner & Blow, 2011). Individuals who experience PTG are able to cope with the trauma through identifying significance or purpose in the traumatic event (Park, Riley, & Snyder, 2012). PTG is ideal as it focuses on the individual experience while acknowledging environmental conditions that reinforced the traumatic event. Outcomes of PTG can include a greater sense of compassion and value towards others; enhanced personal relationships; an overall appreciation of life, including an emphasis on resiliency; higher levels of autonomy; a greater mastery over their environment; more positive relationships; an openness to growth; greater self-acceptance; self-efficacy; internal locus of control; and the belief that they have found their purpose in life (Joseph, Murphy, & Regel, 2012; Sheikh, 2008; Triplett, Tedeschi, Cann, Calhoun, & Reeve, 2012).

The strategies involved in PTG include deliberate rumination, disclosure, and addressing social/cultural factors. Triplett et al. (2012) defined deliberate rumination as a general pattern for deriving meaning from a traumatic event that begins with significant rumination that causes high levels of distress in the individual until a clear resolution of the traumatic event has been achieved. Disclosure consists of identifying the trauma without trying to justify, fix, or change the perspective of the client (Evans, Kluck, Hill, Crumley, & Turchan, 2017; Robertson & Fitzgerald, 1992). Finally, when incorporating PTG approaches, staff should consider the role social support plays in the client's coping style, cognitive processing, and meaning-making expression. Satisfaction with one's social support system has been positively associated with PTG (Linley & Joseph, 2004). Strong social support systems may also be necessary for healthy self-disclosure, another contributing factor for PTG (Lindstrom, Cann, Calhoun, & Tedeschi, 2011). Religious commitment, participating in religious activities, participation in meditative prayer, openness to change, and a willingness to examine challenging questions associated with spirituality has also been positively linked with PTG (Calhoun et al., 2000; Harris et al., 2010; Linley & Joseph, 2004; Shaw, Joseph, & Linley, 2005; Evans, Hemmings, Burkhalter, & Lacy, 2016).

In contrast to the term resilience, the term antifragility has emerged as a way to reframe African American men's response to trauma experienced in American society. Antifragility is beyond resilience. The resilient resists shocks to its system (trauma) and stays the same, while the antifragile gets better. Antifragility has a singular property of allowing us to deal with trauma and volatility of society and still go on to do things without understanding these stressors – and do them well (Taleb, 2012).

Conclusion

Overall, the chapter authors are proud of their and their organizations' work and research with African American fathers. The chapter authors serve as role models for other providers, especially women, in health and social service fields who want to better engage fathers in services. We hope that readers will gain a deeper understanding and desire to change existing systems and practices that exclude African American fathers.

While we strategically developed separate chapters to discuss strategies used with African American fathers who are typically not included in the literature or classroom discussions, it is evident that these fathers' needs and characteristics are not neatly confined to one area. For example, African American fathers experiencing homelessness (Chapter 10) were also in need of mental health services (Chapter 8) and employment (Chapter 3). Some of these fathers were also in need of battering intervention programs (Chapter 9). African American fathers who are in prison (Chapter 5), who are caregivers (Chapter 4), or foster fathers (Chapter 7) may need mental health services. We hope that the work presented by our case contributors will spark discussion and guide practice and programs that address the complex and diverse needs of fathers and support the best outcomes for them and their families.

References

Administration for Children and Families. (2018). *Information memorandum: Integrating approaches that prioritize and enhance father engagement.* Retrieved from https://www.acf. hhs.gov/ofa/resource/acf-acf-im-18-01-integrating-approaches-that-prioritize-and-enhance-father-engagement.

Allen-Meares, P. (1996). Social work services in schools: A look at yesteryear and the future. *Social Work in Education,* 18, 202–208.

Allen-Meares, P., Washington, R.O., & Welsh, B.L. (1996). *Social work services in schools* (2nd ed.). Boston: Allyn & Bacon.

Allport, B.S., Johnson, S., Aqil, A., Labrique, A.B., Nelson, T., Angela, K.C., & Marcell, A.V. (2018). Promoting father involvement for child and family health. *Academic Pediatrics,* 18(7), 746–753.

Bath, H. (2008). The three pillars of trauma-informed care. *Reclaiming Children and Youth,* 17(3), 17–21.

Bauwens, J., & Hourcade, J.J. (1995). *Cooperative teaching: Rebuilding the schoolhouse.* Austin, TX: PRO-ED.

Boardman, T., Catley, D., Grobe, J.E., Little, T.D., & Ahluwalia, J.S. (2006). Using motivational interviewing with smokers: Do therapist behaviors relate to engagement and therapeutic alliance? *Journal of Substance Abuse Treatment,* 31, 329–339.

Borrelli, B., Tooley, E.M., & Scott-Sheldon, L.A. (2015). Motivational interviewing for parent-child health interventions: A systematic review and meta-analysis. *Pediatric Dentistry,* 37(3), 254–265.

Brandon, R.N., & Knapp, M.S. (1999). Interprofessional education and training: Transforming professional preparation to transform human services. *American Behavioral Scientist,* 42(5), 876–891.

Brooks, D. (2011). The limits of empathy. *The New York Times,* 29. Retrieved September 30, 2011, from http://www.nytimes.com/2011/09/30/opinion/brooks-the-limits-of-empathy.html?_r=1.

Brooks, R. (1999). *Empathy: Turning feelings and beliefs into action.* Retrieved from http://www.drrobertbrooks.com/wp/wp-content/uploads/2011/10/Empathy-Turning-Feelings-and-Beliefs-into-Action.pdf.

Butler, C., Rollnick, S., Cohen, D., Bachman, M., Russell, I., & Stott, N. (1999). Motivational consulting versus brief advice for smokers in general practice: A randomized trial. *British Journal of General Practice,* 49, 611–616.

Calhoun, L.G., Cann, A., Tedeschi, R.G., & McMillan, J. (2000). A correlational test of the relationship between posttraumatic growth, religion, and cognitive processing. *Journal of Traumatic Stress: Official Publication of The International Society for Traumatic Stress Studies*, 13(3), 521–527.

Clark, M.D. (2005). Motivational interviewing for the probation staff: Increasing the readiness for change. *Federal Probation*, 69(2), 22–28.

Corrigan, D., & Bishop, K.K. (1997). Creating family-centered integrated service systems and interprofessional educational programs to implement them. *Children & Schools*, 19(3), 149–163.

Courtenay, W. (2011). *Dying to be men: Psychosocial, environmental, and biobehavioral directions in promoting the health of men and boys*. New York: Routledge.

Evans, A.M., Hemmings, C., Burkhalter, C., & Lacy, V. (2016). Responding to race related trauma: Counseling and research recommendations to promote post-traumatic growth when counseling African American males. *The Journal of Counselor Preparation and Supervision*, 8(1), 4.

Evans, A.M., Kluck, A., Hill, D., Crumley, E., & Turchan, J. (2017). Utilizing existential meaning-making as a therapeutic tool for clients affected by poverty. *International Journal of Existential Positive Psychology*, 6(1), 16.

Family Action Centre. (2008). *Framework for father-inclusive practice for early intervention and family-related services*. Australia: The University of Newcastle. Retrieved from www.newcastle.edu.au/centre/fac/efathers/includingfathers.

Franklin, A. J. (1999). Therapeutic support groups for African American men. In L. E. Davis. (Ed,), *Working with African American males: A guide to practice*, (5–14). Oaks, CA: Sage.

Franklin, A. J. (2010). Another side of invisibility: Present and responsible fathers. In C. Z. Oren, & D. C. Oren (Eds.). *Counseling fathers* (121–140). New York: Routledge.

Friend, M., & Cook, L. (2000). *Interactions: Collaboration skills for school professionals*. White Plains, NY: Longman.

Ginsburg, E.H. (1989). *School social work: A practitioner's guide-book: A community-integrated approach to practice*. Springfield, IL: Thomas.

Ginwright, S. (2018). *The future of healing: Shifting from trauma informed care to healing centered engagement*. Occasional Paper, 25, 25–32.

Griffith, D.M., Bruce, M.A., & Thorpe Jr, R.J. (Eds.). (2019). *Men's health equity: A handbook*. Routledge. doi:10.4324/9781315167428.

Harris, J.I., Erbes, C.R., Engdahl, B.E., Tedeschi, R.G., Olson, R.H., Winskowski, A. M. M., & McMahill, J. (2010). Coping functions of prayer and posttraumatic growth. *International Journal for the Psychology of Religion*, 20(1), 26–38.

Hodgkinson, H.L. (1992). *A demographic look at tomorrow*. Washington, DC: Institute for Educational Leadership. (ERIC Document Reproduction Service No. ED 359 087).

Heather, N., Rollnick, S., Bell, A., & Richmond, R. (1996). Effects of brief counselling among male heavy drinkers identified on general hospital wards. *Drug and Alcohol Review*, 15, 29–38.

Hopps, J.G., & Pinderhughes, E. (1999). *Group work with overwhelmed clients: How the power of groups can help people transform their lives*. New York: The Free Press.

Hopps, J.G., Pinderhughes, E., & Shankar, R. (1995). *The power to care: Clinical practice effectiveness with overwhelmed clients*. New York: The Free Press.

Joseph, S., Murphy, D., & Regel, S. (2012). An affective-cognitive processing model of post-traumatic growth. *Clinical Psychology and Psychotherapy*, 19, 316–325.

Julion, W., Gross, D., Barclay-McLaughlin, G., & Fogg, L. (2007). "It's not just about MOMMAS": African-American non-resident fathers' views of paternal involvement. *Research in Nursing & Health*, 30, 595–610.

Ko, J., Ford, D., Kassam-Adams, N., Berkowitz, J., Wilson, C., Wong, M., & Layne, M. (2008). Creating trauma-informed systems: Child welfare, education, first responders, health care, juvenile justice. *Professional Psychology: Research and Practice*, 39(4), 396.

Larner, B., & Blow, A. (2011). A model of meaning-making coping and growth in combat veterans. *Review of General Psychology*, 15(3), 187–197. doi:10.1037/a0024810.

Levinsky, E.R., Forcehimes, A., O'Donohue, W.T., & Beitz, K. (2007). Motivational interviewing: An evidence-based approach to counseling helps patients follow treatment recommendations. *American Journal of Nursing*, 107(10), 50–59.

Lim, C., & Adelman, H. (1997). Establishing school based, collaborative teams to coordinate resources: A case study. *Social Work in Education*, 19(4), 266–278.

Lindstrom, C.M., Cann, A., Calhoun, L.G., & Tedeschi, R.G. (2011). The relationship of core belief challenge, rumination, disclosure, and sociocultural elements to posttraumatic growth. *Psychological Trauma: Theory, Research, Practice, and Policy*, 5, 50–55. doi:10.1037/a0022030.

Linley, P., & Joseph, S. (2004). Positive change following trauma and adversity: A review. *Journal of Traumatic Stress*, 17(1), 11–21. doi:10.1023/B:JOTS.0000014671.27856.7e.

Martinez, K., Rider, F., Cayce, N., Forssell, S., Poirier, J., Hunt, S., & Sawyer, J. (2013). *A guide for father involvement in systems of care*. Washington, DC: Technical Assistance Partnership for Child and Family Mental Health. Retrieved from http://www. tapartnership. org/COP/CLC/publications. php.

Mazza, C. (2002). Young dads: The effects of a parenting program on urban African-American adolescent fathers. *Adolescence*, 37(148), 681–693.

Miller, W.R. (1996). Motivational interviewing: research, practice, and puzzles. *Addictive Behaviors*, 21(6), 835–842.

Miller, W.R., Benefield, R.G., & Tonigan, J.S. (1993). Enhancing motivation for change in problem drinking: a controlled comparison of two therapist styles. *J Consult Clin Psycho*, 61, 455–461.

Miller, W., & Rollnick, S. (1991). *Motivational interviewing: Preparing people to change addictive behavior*. New York: Guilford Press.

Miller, W.R., & Rollnick, S. (2002). *Motivational interviewing: Preparing people for change* (2nd ed.). New York, N.Y., USA: Guilford Press.

Moyers, T.B., & Martin, T. (2006). Therapist influence on client language during motivational interviewing sessions. *Journal of Substance Abuse Treatment*, 30, 245–251.

O'Callaghan, J.B. (1993). *School-based collaboration with families: Constructing family-school-agency partnerships that work*. San Francisco, CA: Jossey-Bass.

Park, C.L., Riley, K.E., & Snyder, L.B. (2012). Meaning making coping, making sense, and post-traumatic growth following the 9/11 terrorist attacks. *The Journal of Positive Psychology*, 7(3), 198–207. doi:10.1080/17439760.2012.671347.

Pearlman, L.A., & Saakvitne, K.W. (1995). *Trauma and the therapist: Countertransference and vicarious traumatization in psychotherapy with incest survivors*. New York: W.W. Norton & Company.

Pruett, M.K., Pruett, K.D., Cowan, C.P., & Cowan, P.A. (2017). Enhancing paternal engagement in a coparenting paradigm. *Child Development Perspectives*, 11(4), 245–250.

Robertson, J. M., & Fitzgerald, L. R. (1992). Overcoming the masculine mystique: Preferences for alternative forms of assistance among men who avoid counseling. *Journal of Counseling Psychology.* 39, 240–246.

Resnicow, K., DiIorio, C., Soet, J.E., Borrelli, B., Hecht, J., & Ernst, D. (2002). Motivational interviewing in health promotion: It sounds like something is changing. *Health Psychology,* 21(5), 444.

Resnicow, K., Jackson, A., Wang, T., Dudley, W., & Baranowski, T. (2001). A motivational interviewing intervention to increase fruit and vegetable intake through Black churches: Results of the Eat for Life Trial. *American Journal of Public Health,* 91, 1686–1693.

Rich, J. (2016). *Moving toward healing: Trauma and violence and boys and young men of color.* Philadelphia, PA: Drexel University School of Public Health.

Rogers, C.R. (1986). Carl Rogers on the development of the person-centered approach. *Person-Centered Review,* 1, 257–259.

Rollins, L.S. (2010). *An exploration of the experiences of African American women who provide direct services to African American nonresidential fathers* (Doctoral dissertation, uga). Retrieved from https://getd.libs.uga.edu/pdfs/rollins_latrice_s_201005_phd.pdf Qu.

Rollnick, S., & Miller, W.R. (1995). What is motivational interviewing? *Behavioural and Cognitive Psychotherapy,* 23, 325–334.

Rostad, W.L., Self-Brown, S., Boyd Jr, C., Osborne, M., & Patterson, A. (2017). Exploration of factors predictive of at-risk fathers' participation in a pilot study of an augmented evidence-based parent training program: A mixed methods approach. *Children and Youth Services Review,* 79, 485–494.

Roy, K. (2008). A life course perspective on fatherhood and family policies in the United States and South Africa. *Fathering: A Journal of Theory Research & Practice about Men as Fathers,* 6(2), 92–112.

Sawyer, A., & Ayers, S. (2009). Post traumatic growth in women after childbirth. *Psychology and Health,* 24(4), 457–471.

Shallcross, L. (2010). Men welcome here. *Counseling Today,* 53, 25–31.

Shannon, S.K., & Abrams, L.S. (2007). Juvenile offenders as fathers: Perceptions of fatherhood, crime, and becoming an adult. *Families in Society,* 88(2), 183–191.

Shaw, A., Joseph, S., & Linley, P. (2005). Religion, spirituality, and posttraumatic growth: A systematic review. *Mental Health, Religion & Culture,* 8(1), 1–11. doi:10.1080/1367467032000157981.

Sheikh, A. (2008). Posttraumatic growth in trauma survivors: Implications for practice. *Counseling Psychology Quarterly,* 21, 85–97.

Simpson, L.R., & Starkey, D.S. (2006). *Secondary traumatic stress, compassion fatigue, and counselor spirituality: Implications for counselors working with trauma.* Retrieved from http://www.counselingoutfitters.com/Simpson.htm.

Sturdivant, M.M., & Byrdsong, R.T. (2013). Mitigating the social and psychological trauma of African American males. In National Association of African American Studies Monograph Series. 1861-1886. *We build our bridges together.* Scarborough, ME. Retrieved from https://www.researchgate.net/profile/Imam_Fauzi/publication/266081245_Analysis_Of_Batechsant_Battery_Technology_Of_Sound_Power_Plant_The_Degree_Of_Micro_Vibration_and_Reverberation_In_Ship_Engine_Room/links/578691e308ae36ad40a6971c/Analysis-Of-Batechsant-Battery-Technology-Of-Sound-Power-Plant-The-Degree-Of-Micro-Vibration-and-Reverberation-In-Ship-Engine-Room.pdf#page=1871.

Sutton, A. (1996). African American men in group therapy. In M.P. Andronico (Ed.), *Men in groups* (pp. 131–150). Washington, DC: American Psychological Association.

Taleb, N. N. (2012). *Antifragile: Things that gain from disorder.* New York: Random House.

Tedeschi, R.G., & Calhoun, L.G. (1995). *Trauma & transformation: Growing in the aftermath of suffering.* Thousand Oaks, CA: Sage Publications.

The Lewin Group (1997). *An evaluability assessment of responsible fatherhood programs: Final report.* Retrieved from http://fatherhood.hhs.gov/evaluaby/intro.htm#TOP.

Thomas, C., Correa, V., & Morsink, C. (1995). *Interactive teaming: Consultation and collaboration in special programs.* Englewood Cliffs, NJ: Merrill.

Trout, J.D. (2010). *Why empathy matters: The science and psychology of better judgment.* New York: Penguin Books.

Tourse, R. W. C., Mooney, J.F., Kline, P., & Davoren, J. (2005). A collaborative model of clinical preparation: A move toward interprofessional field experience. *Journal of Social Work Education, 41*(3), 457–477.

Tourse, R. W. C., & Sulick, J. (1999). The collaborative alliance: Supporting vulnerable children in school. In R. W. C. Tourse & J. Mooney (Eds.), *Collaborative practice: School and human service partnerships* (pp. 57–78). Westport, CT: Praeger.

Triplett, K.N., Tedeschi, R.G., Cann, A., Calhoun, L.G., & Reeve, C.L. (2012). Posttraumatic growth, meaning in life, and life satisfaction in response to trauma. *Psychological Trauma: Theory, Research, Practice, and Policy, 4*(4), 400–410. doi:10.1037/a0024204.

United States Department of Health and Human Services. (2003). *OCSE responsible fatherhood programs: Client characteristics and program outcomes.* Washington, D.C: United States Department of Health and Human Services.

Van Slyke, J. (2013). *Post-traumatic growth. Naval Center for Combat & Operational Stress Control,* 1–5.

Vann, N. (2007). Reflections on the development of fatherhood work. *Applied Developmental Science, 11*(4), 266–268.

Walker, B. (2010). *Spiritual foundation of Maat. Our Weekly Black News.* Retrieved from http://ourweekly.com/news/2010/may/26/spiritual-foundation-of-maat/.

Wilson, A., & Richardson, W. (2020). All I want to say is that they don't really care about us: Creating and maintaining healing-centered collective care in hostile times. *Occasional Paper Series, 2020*(43), 8.

Index

For Product Safety Concerns and Information please contact our EU
representative GPSR@taylorandfrancis.com
Taylor & Francis Verlag GmbH, Kaufingerstraße 24, 80331 München, Germany